Lachs, John

George Santayana

George Santayana

Twayne's United States Authors Series

Kenneth Eble, Editor

University of Utah

TUSAS 536

GEORGE SANTAYANA.
Photography Collection, Harry Ransom Humanities Research Center,
University of Texas at Austin.

George Santayana

By John Lachs

Vanderbilt University

Twayne Publishers
A Division of G.K. Hall & Co. • *Boston*

George Santayana
John Lachs

Copyright 1988 by G.K. Hall & Co.
All rights reserved.
Published by Twayne Publishers
A Division of G.K. Hall & Co.
70 Lincoln Street
Boston, Massachusetts 02111

Copyediting supervised by Barbara Sutton
Book production by Gabrielle B. McDonald
Book design by Barbara Anderson

Typeset in 11 pt. Garamond
by Compset, Inc., Beverly, Massachusetts

Printed on permanent/durable acid-free paper
and bound in the United States of America

Library of Congress Cataloging in Publication Data

Lachs, John.
    George Santayana / by John Lachs.
        p. cm.— (Twayne's United States authors series ; TUSAS 536)
    Bibliography: p.
    Includes index.
    ISBN 0-8057-7517-X (alk. paper)
    1. Santayana, George, 1863–1952. I. Title. II. Series.
B945.S24L28   1988   87-28830
191—dc19   CIP

Contents

About the Author

John Lachs received his B.A. from McGill University. In his senior year he read Santayana's *Scepticism and Animal Faith*; his ensuing fascination with the power and sweep of Santayana's ideas led to a master's thesis at McGill and a doctoral dissertation at Yale. Subsequently, he edited two volumes of Santayana's manuscripts and published articles on virtually all the major areas of Santayana's philosophical thought.

A thinker with broad interests and a practical bent, Lachs is professor of philosophy at Vanderbilt University. He writes on American philosophy and German idealism, on metaphysics and the philosophy of mind, on political philosophy and medical ethics. He has served as president of The Society for the Advancement of American Philosophy and of the C. S. Peirce Society. His *Intermediate Man* (Indianapolis: Hackett, 1981) is an attempt to offer a comprehensive explanation of the problems individuals face in mass society.

Preface

George Santayana made a name for himself as a poet, an essayist, the author of a best-selling novel, and a distinguished teacher. He was celebrated for his perceptive critique of American culture and continues to be viewed, in surprisingly broad circles, as a man of urbane vision or even a modern sage. His prodigious literary production ranged from translations and a play to a remarkable three-volume autobiography. But he was, first and foremost, a philosopher; his systematic ideas about human nature and the world both structured and pervaded all his writing. And he himself maintained that his philosophy was best expressed in the language of the realms of being and of animal faith that he developed after 1920.

Accordingly, my book is restricted to the explication and assessment of this system of thought. Such a focus is necessary, though it entails a cost. Without a clear grasp of Santayana's leading ideas and their interconnection, it is impossible to develop a full understanding even of his novel or his poetry. But attention to the intricacies of his thought leaves no room for exploring his literary work and for the sustained comparison of his mature philosophy with his earlier views. I hope that, although my scope is limited, the value of this systematic exposition of ideas will outweigh its disadvantages. Not only is Santayana's view of the world instructive and beautiful, it also constitutes the key to the structure of his mind. In this way, though I cannot cover the totality of his contribution to American intellectual life, I can at least aim to capture its essence.

Santayana's philosophical ideas represent a viable option for us today. Accordingly, I have refrained from presenting them as historical curiosities. Instead, I have attempted to think with our author, to recreate his edifice of beliefs from the inside. Thoughts are not prunes that acquire value only when dried and dead; they come to nothing unless they are vibrant invitations to expand the mind. Agreement and ultimate truth (if we could ever learn it) are not the primary issues. First we must keep the mind alive, and this is done best by savoring alternatives to our customary modes of thought. Precisely because Santayana challenges some of our most sacred dogmas, his views must be welcomed as life-giving intellectual fare.

Throughout the book, I have made special efforts to explain abstract philosophical points in generally accessible language. Although specialists may profit from the work, advanced training in philosophy is not required for understanding it. The chapters follow a natural line of development from Santayana's rejection of skepticism through the successive phases of building a complete philosophy of animal faith. The continuity and interconnectedness of the ideas suggest the unity of the system; the whole, once grasped, reveals itself as a sweeping and consistent vision of the world and of our place and prospects in it.

Many years ago, I completed a lengthy manuscript on Santayana's philosophy. Along with all the rest of our luggage, with my notes and my books, it was stolen out of our car on a sabbatical trip. It took me a very long time to return to writing on Santayana again. I am grateful to Twayne Publishers for waiting patiently until a new book was ready to emerge. Without their understanding, this volume, whatever its merits, would not exist.

John Lachs

Vanderbilt University

Chronology

1863   Jorge Agustín Nicolás Santayana, son of Josefina Borrás Sturgis and Agustín Santayana, born on 16 December, in Madrid, Spain.

1872   Travels with his father to join his mother in Boston. His father returns to Avila, Spain.

1874–1882   Attends Boston Latin School.

1880   Receives Poetry Prize at Boston Latin School.

1882   Enters Harvard University.

1886   Receives B.A. summa cum laude. Shares with his friend C. A. Strong the Walker Fellowship for graduate study in Germany.

1886–1888   Travels in Europe and studies in Berlin.

1889   Completes doctoral dissertation at Harvard on *Lotze's System of Philosophy*. Accepts appointment at Harvard as instructor of philosophy.

1893   Father dies.

1894   First book, *Sonnets and Other Verses,* is published.

1896   *The Sense of Beauty.*

1896–1897   On leave from Harvard, studies at King's College, Cambridge, and discusses philosophy with Bertrand Russell, G. E. Moore, and J. M. E. McTaggart.

1898   Promoted to assistant professor at Harvard.

1900   *Interpretations of Poetry and Religion.*

1904–1906   Travels in Europe and the Middle East.

1905–1906   *The Life of Reason; Or, The Phases of Human Progress* (5 volumes).

1907   Promoted to professor at Harvard.

1912   Mother dies. He resigns his professorship to devote full time to literary pursuits.

1914–1919   Settles in Oxford.

1915   *Egotism in German Philosophy.*

1920–1941   Regular round of travels in France, Spain, Italy, and Switzerland.

1920   *Character and Opinion in the United States.*

1923   *Scepticism and Animal Faith.*

1925   *Dialogues in Limbo.*

1927   Meets David Cory, who becomes his secretary and later his literary executor. *The Realm of Essence.*

1930   *The Realm of Matter.*

1932   Declines offer to become William James professor at Harvard.

1935–1936   Only novel, *The Last Puritan,* is published and becomes a Book-of-the-Month Club best-seller.

1937   *The Realm of Truth.*

1940   *The Realm of Spirit.*

1941   Moves into a nursing home operated by the Blue Sisters, an order of nuns, in Rome.

1944   *Persons and Places,* the first volume of his autobiography.

1945   *The Middle Span,* the second volume of his autobiography.

1945–1950   Enjoys visits in Rome from American servicemen and intellectuals familiar with his work.

1946   *The Idea of Christ in the Gospels; Or, God in Man.*

1951   *Dominations and Powers.*

1952   Dies in Rome, of stomach cancer, on 26 September.

1953   *My Host the World,* the third volume of his autobiography, published posthumously.

1953–1969   Various volumes of previously unpublished writings appear in print.

1986   First volume of new, authoritative *Collected Works* appears.

Chapter One
Life and Thought
What Makes Philosophy Worthwhile?

What makes a philosopher significant in modern life? Is there anything beyond antiquarian interest to justify the hours one has to invest in studying his thought? These are questions rarely asked; yet they are frequently answered in our practice. For philosophers are no longer read by a general audience. And, as if to return the favor or perhaps as a measure of self-defense, philosophers no longer even attempt to write for the average man.

The growth in the professionalization of philosophy has been accompanied by an increase in its vacuousness and irrelevance. Precision yields results in philosophy no less than in science. But the findings of science are translated by technology into aids to better life. There is no comparable application of the fruits of philosophical labor. Contemporary thinkers prefer to deal with topics of high abstraction; in the process of honing their instrument they tend to forget the primary aim of philosophy. Logic and the theory of knowledge command the attention of some of our best minds; too many of those who write on ethics and political philosophy focus on the piecemeal study of clear but abstract principles without any attempt to apply them to the murky facts.

Doing philosophy is intrinsically enjoyable. Yet there is an ultimate hollowness to all thought that is not an instrument for improving life. In this sense, the value of philosophy is ultimately moral in the broadest sense of this term. It aids us in understanding the world and our place in it. In the end, it must make an impact upon what manner of persons we are and how we live. It is this moral payoff of systematic thought that is frequently forgotten by systematic thinkers today. Philosophers have moved inside the ivory tower, flooded the moat, and cranked up the drawbridge of communication. Each year a few graduate students are allowed to swim across, but they must promise not to let anything they learn make a difference to how they want to live.

1

Santayana the Academic

George Santayana is a refreshing exception to this trend in academic philosophy. He was an academic himself, having earned a doctorate from Harvard University in 1889. He taught philosophy at Harvard for more than twenty years. Yet he never became a scholar in the narrow sense. His life always overflowed the restrictive banks of the university. His desires were not those of the academic denizen, his opinions were not shaped by the dead orthodoxy of the day. He thought freely and with a courage that was rare even in the days when the freethinker could expect the compliments of anger and retaliation. In our age, when the unorthodox in thought or behavior receive little but neglect, even perversity ceases to be a motive for dissent. For us, only the grim determination to be autonomous remains and perhaps the satisfaction of thinking of ourselves as kin to those minds that faced a public lie and clung to truth though it cost them their lives.

Historically, Santayana's ability to resist the popular opinions of his day was probably grounded in the fact that, having been born in Spain in 1863, he was moved by his mother from his beloved Avila to Boston at the age of nine. He never quite learned to find himself at home in the cold climate of Boston and the early exposure to two radically divergent cultures enabled him to view each in perspective. Like an amphibian, he could move in two worlds. Neither was alien, yet each was seen clearly with its flaws and limits. This early exposure to different ways may well have been the psychological groundwork of his later relativism. It was indubitably the source of his astounding ability to view all things, even those that related to him immediately, from a detached perspective.

Too deep an involvement in a culture or in daily affairs makes vision difficult. Yet the tendency to view all things at a distance, as though by reversing our binoculars, gives others the impression of being without feeling. Bertrand Russell once said of Santayana that he was "a cold fish." The injustice of this characterization, particularly by Russell, is poignant. Russell, focusing on appearances, knew little of his friend's generosity. He could not have known that when he was in financial difficulties during the 1930s, Santayana was the anonymous donor of a large sum to bail him out. Such generosity was commonplace with Santayana; he was ready to share with friends whatever his fortune had provided. He supported Daniel Cory, a young man just out of college who sought him out in 1927, for the last twenty-five years of his life.

The support continued even after Santayana died in 1952; he gave Cory all the income from his copyrights and left him a trunk of manuscripts, which Cory sold little by little. There is rich evidence in Santayana's letters, both published and unpublished, that he was always ready to help with advice or money whenever his friends needed it.

His Character

The combination of detached vision and a warm heart gives us a clue to much of Santayana's complex character and philosophy. His life and his work are both unities wrought with difficulty out of opposites. In his philosophy he attempted to combine straightforward materialism with a tender insistence on the value of the spiritual life. He was deeply convinced that the individual was the ultimate source of everything valuable, yet he showed a sensitive appreciation of the role of social life. He admired the works of imagination and intellect, yet he also believed that the mind was an impotent spectator of the flow of events. He denied the literal truth of all religion while retaining a keener sense for the symbolic power of his native, unpracticed, Catholicism than many churchgoing Catholics.

His character itself was riddled with contradictions. From 1889 to 1912, his years of employment in the philosophy department at Harvard, he taught with the energy and enthusiasm that make for classroom success, yet he never found his lectures fulfilling. He was naturally open-minded and gregarious, yet his social contacts showed him to be guarded and retiring. Beauty attracted him and as a dashing, fiery-eyed Spaniard he was attractive to many a beauty in Cambridge and Boston, yet there is no evidence left to us of any romantic involvement on his part. Santayana lived a life of deep private significance doing what he wanted, creating what he thought was beautiful and good, yet a deep pessimism pervaded his thought, if not his moods. Both before and after his early retirement from Harvard, he traveled widely and knew the cities, the history, and the culture of countries on two continents, yet he always thought of himself as a guest in this world, not someone who is at home.

His Private Personality

It is difficult to plumb the depths of Santayana's private personality. He believed that the person objectifies and universalizes himself in his work: in the process of converting private conviction and personal pain into a work of art, the individuality and privacy drop out. The public persona covers the private man the way clothes cover the body. Here and there we discover a hint of what might lie beneath, but everything is a matter of guesswork or risky inference. This guardedness itself, of course, tends to increase our fascination with the man; interest is more intense and more sustained when clothes are provocatively worn than in a nudist colony. Yet even Santayana's autobiography, published in three volumes near the end of his long life, is disappointing to those who want to get inside his privacy. It is an account of his perception of the places he has seen and the persons he has known. The perceiver rarely appears and when he does it is only as a formal, public self.

Interestingly enough, even Santayana's voluminous correspondence reveals relatively little. His letters, written to both important and insignificant people, are full of wisdom and philosophy. They show compassion and good sense. But they say very little about their author, except for the briefest accounts of what he does and a few hints of how he feels. If there ever was a man who should have known him, it was his longtime secretary, disciple, and friend, Daniel Cory. Yet even Cory failed to penetrate to the personal core. Given their intimate friendship of over two decades, his book on Santayana is distressingly thin on personal details.

It may well be, of course, that the search for an inner man in Santayana is a wild goose chase. Admittedly, he had close ties to his mother and he loved his sister, Susanna, in an unwavering and intense way throughout her life. There are substantial collections of letters, such as those to the poet Robert Lowell, which will not be accessible to the public for many years, that may reveal hitherto unsuspected realms of personal involvement. These considerations notwithstanding, however, it is clear that Santayana did not allow himself the opportunity for an intensely developed personal existence. He never married, had no children, kept up with few of his students, minimized close friendships and involvements by his retiring attitude, and kept no diaries of his private reflections. Much of his internal life was transmuted into public philosophy. Throughout his long existence, he was deeply engaged in writing. His poetry, his drawings, his translations, his systematic philosophical works took up most of his time. Perhaps by conscious design, he allowed little time for the flowering of a private self. He enjoyed listening to music, seeing beautiful scenes, and being absorbed in contemplation. But these activities were, by his own account, nothing private: in the enjoyment of beauty and in thought we break through, he believed, to a world of essences or themes that serve as a medium for uniting minds.

Santayana, the public man, was primarily a writer. Although he lived through two world wars, without participating in either, his life was uneventful. His years at Boston Latin School naturally took him to Harvard, where he entered as an undergraduate in 1882. Upon completing a dissertation on the German philosopher Herman Lotze, he was invited to join the Harvard faculty. He was promoted to professor in 1907, but in 1912, in spite of efforts to keep him there, he resigned and moved to Europe. For the remaining forty years of his long life, he traveled in England, France, Italy, and Spain, living in small hotel rooms and reading and writing constantly. In this period, he published almost twenty books and filled a steamer trunk with his unpublished essays, drafts, and notes. He took little interest in the life of the communities where he lived and none in political activity. The significant dates in his existence were almost all dates of his publications. His last years were spent in Rome, where he continued his literary work until a few weeks before his death in 1952.

His Teachers

Santayana had distinguished teachers at Harvard and distinguished colleagues when he himself taught there. William James, the great philosopher and psychologist, took an active interest in the young man and helped him obtain his faculty appointment. James's attitude to Santayana was ambivalent: he had a warm concern and admiration for the man combined with a cordial disdain for his philosophy. He focused on the scholastic elements in Santayana's thought to such an extent that he failed to note the immense impact his own *Principles of Psychology* had made on all of the younger man's subsequent works.

The idealist Josiah Royce was another colleague of Santayana's at Harvard. His assessment of Royce's thought in *Character and Opinion in the United States* is perhaps the most devastating critique of that philosopher written to this day. Santayana's treatment of James in his autobiography shows the same intellectual instinct for the jugular. But here Santayana manifests a savage insight not only into the thought but also into the personality of his subject. James's foibles and idiosyncrasies are exposed in a way in which no one has yet and probably no one ever will expose Santayana's more guarded but perhaps no less eccentric personality.

His Students and Influence

Santayana had the privilege of educating an entire generation of philosophers. R. B. Perry, C. I. Lewis, Durant Drake, W. P. Montague, Frederick Woodbridge and many other stars in the philosophical firmament of this country in the first half of the twentieth century either went through his classes or were taught by professors who did. His influence in American philosophy was established with the publication of his first book, *The Sense of Beauty*, in 1896. The five volumes of his *The Life of Reason* (1905–06) were used as a bible by American naturalists. Although he left his teaching post in 1912, and went to Europe never to return, his influence in this country did not reach its height until the 1920s and 1930s. During those decades his books were widely read and studied; the *Journal of Philosophy*, the major philosophical publication of the day, frequently published his articles; courses of study in colleges and universities routinely included his works.

World War II found Santayana old but philosophically still vigorous in Italy. Cut off from funds and from his intellectual outlets in the United States, he retired to the safety of a convent in Rome. Though there was considerable interest in the expatriate sage after the arrival in Rome of Allied forces, he never regained much philosophical influence in America. Since his death, there has been a slow increase of interest in his work. Many of his better known books are now available in paperback. Graduate students are, once again, writing dissertations on the technical aspects of his philosophy. An increasing number of undergraduate courses utilize his major, and in some cases his posthumously published, works. Most important of all, many thoughtful laymen read his writings for their intrinsic beauty as well as the moral enlightenment they convey.

Intellectual Heritage

Santayana's intellectual heritage is genuinely cosmopolitan. His works show a complete mastery of the philosophical classics. But his reading was far more extensive than even this. He was thoroughly acquainted with the great works of literature of both East and West. He read voluminously in four or five languages and kept abreast of the best scholarly writing of his day. He studied the great works of religion in painstaking detail: his *The Realm of Spirit* shows extensive familiarity with Buddhist and Hindu sources, and he turned himself into an expert on the Bible in preparation for his *The Idea of Christ in the Gospels*. He was well aware of the scientific developments of his day and formed his philosophy in such a way as to make no claim concerning the physical structure of man or the world. He thought it the function of science to determine the facts about nature as best as such facts may be known by human beings; philosophy and religion were to yield to empirical investigation concerning facts, even though they retained their supremacy in the moral sphere.

In spite of his acquaintance with the broad outlines of science, Santayana gladly proclaimed himself "an ignorant man, almost a poet."[1] This is no overstatement or false humility. The heart of science is in its details, and Santayana never had any interest in the narrow specifics of the physical order. He thought that scientific views would come and go with the passage of time. He lacked the mathematical background to comprehend them and the sustaining interest in minutiae to permit him to get absorbed in them. His belief in the autonomy of science functioned like a double-edged sword. On the one hand, it served to control the excesses of philosophers in trying to compete with science on the basis of mere speculation or moral demands. On the other hand, however, it placed sharp limits on the scope of science, restricting its valid application to the sphere of nature alone. By ceding matter to science, Santayana felt liberated from having to attend to the details of either. He felt he could concentrate on the investigation of the moral life.

His Philosophical Style

This relative inattention to detail also shows itself in Santayana's treatment of philosophical themes. In his opinion, philosophy is not the science of careful argument but the art of vision. His attempt was to focus on what he called "the large facts," the main rhythms and requirements of nature as they affect human life and personality. There are few explicit arguments in his philosophical works. It is not that he paid no heed to carefulness and precision in thought. On the contrary, his philosophical system has a remarkable unity and coherence. It is just that he thought arguments were like the beams that hold up a house; while essential to a sound structure, they are not to be displayed as decoration or as the furniture of rooms. As a result, only the conclusions of his arguments appear in his books. The arguments themselves can be reconstructed, but in his view their only value is utilitarian.

Santayana's philosophical heritage fully reflects his own commitment to philosophy as articulate vision. As a graduate student and in later years he studied the arguments of others carefully. It is reported that when an impertinent priest attempted to bring Santayana back into the fold by arguments of a Thomist persuasion, the old philosopher quoted him the details of the view from Aquinas in Latin. Much as he was at home with arguments, he felt no temptation to follow those who developed their philosophy in lockstep with the march of reasoning. He thought that arguments could rage forever on each contested principle or view. No philosophical position could ever be supported to the satisfaction of the opposing camp. In the end, everything would hang on our basic principles and personal commitments. It is not that these cannot be criticized; on the contrary, they must be if one's philosophy is to escape the fate of "dreaming in words."[2] But any such critique must itself presuppose some ultimate principles as yet uncriticized. He argues in the first chapter of *Scepticism and Animal Faith* that there is no indubitable starting point, no first principle of criticism. As a result, there can be no certainty and no agreement in philosophy.

It is better, Santayana thinks, if philosophers own up to the true nature of their enterprise and abandon all pretense of scientific precision, evidential adequacy, or universal truth. The task of the thinker is to "clean the windows of his soul,"[3] to evoke the most general of essences for moral enlightenment. The chief issue, he says in the eloquent preface to *Scepticism and Animal Faith,* is "the relation of man and of his spirit to the universe."[4] Given the variety in human nature and the immensity of the topic, it is no accident that philosophers fail to agree and fall shy of ultimate truth. The truth itself will depend at least partly on the soul whose windows we must clean. If we take this simple notion to heart, all moral knowledge at once stands revealed as relative, and philosophy becomes a mode of self-expression.

These convictions justify Santayana, at least in his own eyes, in painting with a broad brush. His treatment of philosophical topics may appear sketchy at times; this, he thinks, is due not to lack of care on his part but to the fact that on certain subjects the human mind is not in a position to know much. We can think of transition or change only "as a transformation of one thing into another, involving two natural moments, and leaving the bond between them obscure."[5] On the issue of the ultimate nature of matter (as an ontological, not a scientific category), he loudly declares that no enlightenment is possible: this ultimate principle of existence is like the whirlwind whose effects we see but whose inner nature is inaccessible to mind.

As a result of his conviction that arguments fail to convince and details are inaccessible or fail to satisfy, many of Santayana's works constitute descriptions and redescriptions of his system as a whole. The accounts are remarkably consistent throughout. The variations in his expression of the same ideas are rarely at odds with one another; on the contrary, they are helpful in understanding his real intent. But, on the whole, later statements tend frequently to be but alternatives to the earlier ones without constituting any real advance. This, once again, may be justified by Santayana's belief that philosophy communicates not by disclosing facts but by evoking visions. In this light, we may think of the alternative descriptions of his system as varied stimuli intended to engage a variety of minds.

His Relation to Plato

This feature of Santayana's philosophy, along with many others, brings to mind his similarity to Plato. Plato's deepest doctrine was also that philosophical enlightenment could not be taught but only evoked. His impatience with the poets was perhaps a family feud; he himself became a poet the moment he moved past mundane arguments and neared the ultimate. Plato's conviction that we have only myths to convey the profound insights literal language cannot convey appears to have been generalized by Santayana into a view of all language and thought. For him, language, a human creation, functions as an instrument in the service of cognition and, in the end, of life. It never captures the essence of its object. Language is always symbolic; its adequacy is measured by how well it expresses the thoughts of the speaker or how well it enables us to grasp and use the object it reveals. A description, then, is not like a flashlight that discloses the corner of a room the way it *is*. It is closer to the vision of the jaundiced man, in which the internal state of the agent and his instrument are inseparably reflected in the object.

Santayana also agrees with Plato that there are real forms or structures without which nothing could exist. Plato thought of these forms as the prototypes of natural kinds and attributes: there was a form of man and a form of dog and a form of oak tree, as well as forms for justice, wisdom, and virtue. These forms or universals existed, in Plato's opinion, both as structures and as standards for the objects in our everyday world. Ordinary objects could exist only by "participating in" or borrowing their nature from these eternal, unchanging essences. Yet, at the same time, existing entities always fell short of fully manifesting the nature of the perfect forms. The measure of the faithfulness with which a changing thing displayed its proper form was at once the measure of its perfection. The aim of everything that inhabits this twilight world of ours was to become more nearly what it can and ought to be, viz. a perfect thing of its kind or a full embodiment of its form.

Plato thought of these forms as general in nature. There was only one form of man. Each of us participated in this form to a greater or lesser extent. The more nearly we approximated to this ideal of what a man should be, to true humanity, the more perfect we would be. The standards existed eternally and altogether independently of the world or of our minds. If anything, they served as necessary conditions of the existence of ourselves and of the things around us. But nothing we could do would affect them; they were simply forms available for shaping the world, if only the world would adopt them for the purpose.

Santayana studied Plato and Aristotle intensively at Cambridge in England, when he took an academic year's leave in 1896–97. He was deeply impressed by Plato's treatment of universals but at the same time found himself repelled by the moral absolutism into whose service Plato, the social reformer, pressed them. Why should we suppose, Santayana asked himself, that forms are restricted to a small number, each endowed with moral prerogatives? In Plato's dialogue *Parmenides,* the young Socrates is depicted as balking at the thought that there might be ideal forms for hair and dirt and mud. Why, Santayana demanded to know, should we not say that every actual and every conceivable property and relation and thing has a corresponding form or essence? And, most important, why should we suppose that there is only one form of humanity, implying that there is but one manner in which human life may be perfected?

The democratic pluralism Santayana learned from William James showed itself quickly at this crucial juncture in his philosophical development. He could not make himself believe that all human psyches were of one sort, that everyone worthy of being called human would have to share identical values. He saw hints even in Plato that human life might find fulfillment in a variety of different ways. In the *Republic,* Plato distinguished three classes of individuals; members of each pursued happiness in their own divergent ways. Persons of desire found fulfillment in the production, consumption, and accumulation of worldly goods; persons of courage sought excitement in action and adventure; persons of wisdom gained their satisfaction in knowledge and the attendant well-ordered life. Of course, what Plato gave with one hand he took away with the other: he thought that these types of human beings were themselves aligned in an order of ultimate perfection. The persons of philosophical wisdom constituted the closest approximation to what a human being should be; the consumer was a poor, distorted actualization of human potentiality. Santayana could not in good conscience believe this. It is not that he had a high regard for the man who spent his life scratching his itches or consuming beyond his needs. But he did have a vivid moral imagination and this enabled him to place himself in the shoes of others who lived by alien values.

The empathy for alien souls, without a personal identification with their goals, enabled him to appraise others more justly than do fervent moralists. If the essence of humanity is what makes us human, is there no essence that makes us individually who we are? If forms are to be conceived as features or characteristics, no matter how complex, each of us must have a unique essence. Each person must, then, be a perfect exemplification of himself, and if he changes, then a perfect replica of the new essence he assumes.

An Infinity of Individual Essences

This single move from the generic essence of mankind to specific essences for individuals radicalizes Santayana's philosophy. For the moment each of us is viewed as fully embodying an essence, forms cease to function as standards of perfection. Nothing can serve as a standard if we cannot fail to live up to it; since in at least one sense we cannot be but who we are, our form will structure us without providing a guide for action or a goal to reach. In a more careful analysis of the moral life later on, Santayana reintroduces an account of how our natures demand certain actions and of how individual moral failure is possible. But the rejection of Plato's claim that forms are generic at once prepares the ground for Santayana's moral relativism.

It also opens the door to an actual infinity of essences. If each characteristic or feature of every existent is an essence, there is literally no end to the essences there are. We can see how essences must be infinite in number in a variety of ways. If each number is an essence, evidently essences must be infinitely numerous. Similarly, even if there are only a finite number of things in the world, each can be seen to have an infinite number of properties in the following way. No item is identical with any one of its features, f. This is evidently true, and it immediately generates another property, namely that of not being identical with f. The item is, of course, also not identical with the property of not being identical with f. This generates another property, and so on, ad infinitum. Another way to get to the idea that essences must be infinite may start by viewing the entire history of the world as a monstrously complex essence. Each change in this complex essence, no matter how minute, generates a different total essence. Since essences differ if any of their constituents or the order of their constituents differ, the most insignificant imagined change of the minutest event makes for a different total world-essence. There is no limit to the changes that are conceivable in this way, and each of them yields a slightly different possible world.

Santayana's indebtedness to Plato, then, is extensive. It is by reflecting on the Platonic realm of forms that Santayana came up with two of his most characteristic and most remarkable philosophical views. The infinite realm of essence is conceived by him as enjoying the same ontological status as Plato's realm of forms. Each essence is eternally and changelessly self-identical. Each serves as a possible character of existence, but has a sort of being which is independent of nature and of mind. And Santayana's moral relativism is clearly connected to his rejection of Plato's view that as a result of generic forms, existence falls into natural species. The proliferation of human natures opens the door to an individualism that is as radical as any found in the annals of philosophy.

His Debt to Aristotle

Santayana's debt to Aristotle is no less evident that the Platonic traces in his thought. The entire tone of Santayana's moral philosophy is Aristotelian. The sharp contrast between moral and intellectual virtue becomes in Santayana the distinction between the life of reason and the spiritual life. The Greek notion of reason as moderating and harmonizing the passions is prominently present in Santayana's account of the moral life. And the topics treated in Aristotle's great *Nicomachean Ethics* not only recur in a number of Santayana's books, but virtually each discussion of them reflects Aristotle's arguments or conclusions

Aristotle's influence is most pronounced, however, in the basic categories in terms of which Santayana chose to think. For one, Santayana was satisfied that individual existents were composites of matter and form. The form, of course, was an essence selected for embodiment from among an infinity of alternatives. Matter was conceived by him as the sheer, irrational thrust of existence,[6] "the insane emphasis" that accrued to certain essences. Since no essence could render itself or another existent, essences could not account for the raw energy or selective force of the material component. Matter, for Santayana, had no intrinsic properties at all; at any rate, no conceivable feature of it could account for the role it plays in the world. Viewed in this light, Santayana's matter closely resembles Aristotle's prime matter or pure potentiality. I say that the two notions closely resemble one another instead of being identical because Aristotle thought of the potential as somehow passive, while Santayana maintains that matter is the sole source of existence and activity. This last disagreement is of central importance for Santayana's metaphysics: it is what makes him a materialist who denies any efficacy to essence and to mind. Apart from this difference, however, Santayana agrees with Aristotle that matter in its purity is the faceless counterpart of form.

Santayana also borrows from Aristotle the concept of activity. Activity in this sense is contrasted with process and differs widely from what we normally understand by the word "action." In its simplest signification it is something we do for its own sake. Since in such cases we aim simply at what we do, there is no distinction between the means and the end we intend, between the doing and the deed that is accomplished. Such activity represents something that is self-contained, something that aims at no product beyond itself. It is on this model that Santayana conceived of mind. Consciousness, he thought, is a dead end in the causal processes of nature. It is an activity in Aristotle's sense, the second actuality of a natural body. This flowering of human organic processes is both an end product without further issue and an end in itself, and as such intrinsically valuable.

This conception of mind suggests that Santayana's ultimate view of nature was framed not in the terms of modern science but in those of potentialities actualized. He thought of existence simply as actualized potentiality and of matter as the indefinite potentiality of all things. There is evidence that he believed causation itself was but a process that converts potentialities into act, albeit in a way that necessarily remains hidden to the mind.[7]

His Relation to Science

Reflection on this approach to a philosophy of nature might suggest that Santayana failed to profit from the advances of modern science. In a sense, this is absolutely true. In one place he remarks that in his youth there was widespread belief in "sovereign laws" of nature and in the ultimate adequacy of science to discover them.[8] All of this seems to have fallen apart later, following the contributions of Einstein and Heisenberg to physical theory, combined perhaps with a better understanding of the nature of the scientific enterprise. In Santayana's work there is little reference to the findings of science. The scientists in whom he shows an interest, such as Freud, deal largely with psychological matters, matters that are of importance to Santayana because of their bearing on the nature of man. Physical theory interests him relatively little: he thinks it too far from the central task of philosophy, which is an exploration of the nature of the good life.

But there is an even deeper reason for Santayana's return to what we may think are prescientific categories. In the end, science has not succeeded and cannot succeed in revealing to us the mystery of existence. We can learn more and more about the physical structures that surround us and such knowledge is superbly useful for the manipulation of the environment. But it never penetrates below the level of conjunctions and lawlike regularities. The bafflement of the primitive man at existence itself, at seeing anything come into being or recede into nothingness, stays with us in spite of everything science tells us about the world. Scientists attempt to show how one type of event causes another by interposing a third sort of occurrence between the two; ingesting a poison is supposed to cause death by immobilizing the muscles or the lungs. But such an account misses the ultimate mystery that surrounds the generation of anything. No matter how many types of events are interposed between the cause and the effect, the problem of how one can go from the first event to the very next, no matter how close or how similar to it, remains unsolved. How can anything ever give rise to anything else? Though science may provide us with an exhaustive account of the details of change, the ordinary man and the philosopher will end up no less baffled by the metaphysical problem

4

of how life and death, how coming into being and passing away, how change itself is possible.

The categories of potentiality and actuality are thought by Santayana to be less alien to the ordinary mind than the language of laws and functions employed in the sciences. These categories, frankly interpreted, forever remind us that we do not understand. They are adequate to summarize the patterns and tendencies of human nature and of the human world. Beyond that, they do and pretend to do nothing. This lack of pretense is itself a boon; at least we avoid the temptation of supposing that we can be omniscient or that science will meet all human needs and eliminate the symbolic life of the mind, religion and philosophy. Santayana's return to Aristotelian categories, then, is not an attempt to deny the usefulness or the validity of science. It is, on the contrary, the result of an effort to put science in its proper, human context so that we may celebrate it without illusions and live without becoming its dupes.

This notion of the ultimate metaphysical inadequacy of science reminds one of the attitude of Schopenhauer. In differentiating the physical world of space, time, and causal connections from the underlying, primordial world of will, Schopenhauer explicitly limited science to the exploration of the laws of phenomena. The ultimately real world of will was one to which each of us could have internal access. It made for all the change that occurred in the physical world but could itself never be captured by an external method of investigation. Santayana himself flirted with using the terms "will" and "primal will" to designate the ultimate generative principle of all things. This is not an unattractive designation; the word "will" suggests just the sort of unpredictable, creative energy that seems to underlie the world. But Santayana clearly disagrees with Schopenhauer on the issue of access to this force; though he thinks that it runs through our bodies, he is convinced that we can have no cognitive contact with it at all. And there is a further disagreement if calling matter "will" is taken too literally or in too mentalistic a way. For Santayana thinks there is little reason to believe that this primordial energy resembles anything conscious or mental. It is gregarious in hurrying from form to form, but it has no purpose, no intelligence, no aim.

His Pessimism

This comparison with Schopenhauer naturally leads to another. Much has been made of Santayana's pessimism. Many have supposed that the primary thrust of his philosophy is not so much to free us from illusions as to express disillusionment. Those who believe this naturally take the spiritual life to be one of self-abnegation, a transcendence of the world that amounts to its ultimate rejection. If Santayana really thought this, he would be very close indeed to Schopenhauer's pessimism. He would then think that, when all is said and done, life is not worth living, that frustration is the inescapable fate of every living creature.

But this is surely a misapprehension of Santayana's intent and vision. It is true that he has few illusions about life and none about its ultimate outcome. He has an almost stoic commitment to facing the facts with all the equanimity a finite mind can muster. But this inner calm in the teeth of possible disaster and certain death should not, he believes, take anything from the joy of living. On the contrary, such realism about our prospects should enhance our enjoyments, while such enjoyments are still available. The rejection of immortality and the acceptance of the relativity and evanescence of values have traditionally been associated with philosophies that advocated an abundant life within our finite scope. Lucretius, the French philosophes of the eighteenth century, and freethinkers of all ages have found a modest view of human hopes compatible with joy in the exercise of human faculties. Death may well be our destiny, but rest and sleep are premature at noon.

The Spiritual Life

But, it may be argued, Santayana advocates a spiritual life which, by his own account, is a disintoxication from values. In such an existence, nothing is loved, nothing is chosen, nothing is rejected. The result is a passivity that extends to every element of life, a passivity which in the end makes it impossible to choose even life over death.

This argument suffers from two weaknesses, both of them fatal. The first is the supposition that Santayana advocates the spiritual life. In fact, he is too much of a relativist to prescribe for others or even to attempt to persuade them. His intention is primarily to describe a perfection possible for some humans; there is no indication that he wishes to pass judgment on it. Second, the spiritual life is not a life-style.[9] It is not, as it has often been supposed to be, a rival to the life of reason. Rightly understood, it is a sort of special fulfillment that is possible within the life of reason and within other forms of life. Its essence is precisely that it does not shape an existence. It could never do that. It is simply the sum of those moments in an individual's life in which animal care is transcended and the soul is absorbed in the contemplation of the immediate. Such contemplation is frequently described as joyous, as a rapture. It is much closer to the truth if we think of it not as a valueless act but as a consummation, an activity, an act that is its own end.

On this reading, Santayana is not a pessimist about the internal meaning and the daily possibilities of human existence. The ultimate futility of it all stands as but an insignificant terminal point that is unable to rob us of what we have. If we think of the world as our host, there is no reason to stop the feast because the time will come when we will have overstayed our welcome.

Santayana on Skepticism

The similarity between Descartes and Santayana has also been exaggerated. To be sure, the first hundred pages of *Scepticism and Animal Faith* mimic Descartes's method of doubt. But here the similarity ends. Descartes's systematic doubt was designed to uncover the certain and indubitable first principles of human knowledge. Descartes knew very well what these principles were; as soon as he got near them by means of his skeptical method, his jaundiced eye was left behind and he was happy to develop the uncritical edifice of his favorite dogmas. By contrast, Santayana's skepticism is unrelenting. Descartes's belief that we know the self with certainty is instantly dissolved by critical scrutiny. As it turns out, no certain principles of human knowledge are discovered; the skeptical enterprise resolutely carried out leaves the human mind bankrupt. The lesson to be learned is not that if we free our minds of cant, we shall at last see clearly and discover the proper objects of human knowledge. On the contrary, if we eliminate all belief, interpretation, and conjecture, we are left with no knowledge at all. The only thing left is the riskless certainty of a spread of objects contemplated but not understood.

So whereas the skeptical method led Descartes to assurance, it moved Santayana only in the direction of his conviction that it is unreasonable to expect any knowledge to be certain. The result is his rejection of the very criterion which sets all of us on the search for incontrovertible knowing. Santayana thinks that the rationalist principle which demands that nothing be dignified by the name knowledge unless it is capable of rigid proof sets unrealistic standards for our life and station. Such a criterion may be appropriate to a disembodied mind intent upon intuiting truth or deducing true descriptions of the universe. But it is altogether unworkable for the animal engaged in action, for the mind bound to special organs and violent perspectives in a changing world.

Skepticism, for Santayana, is an intellectual exercise. It is useful because it helps us discover the ultimate objects of consciousness and because it reveals the bankruptcy of rigid standards of reason. It leads us to the insight that long before we are minds, we are bodies engaged in the give and take of a difficult environment. The standards of knowledge must, therefore, grow naturally out of the demands imposed upon us by the need for intelligent action. Viewed in this light, Santayana appears as a direct descendant of those German philosophers who maintained the primacy of action over thought. We can also see why he properly belongs with other American philosophers as a pragmatist of sorts.

This reading of the point of Santayana's skeptical reduction is resisted by some interpreters. They prefer to think that our philosopher is in fact a skeptic who settles for animal faith as only a second best, as something that has value only as a distorted replica of what knowledge ought to be. From the perspective of the rationalist criterion of knowledge, this is an accurate characterization. If certainty is our aim, animal belief will always be a poor substitute. But this conception presupposes what Santayana explicitly denies: the validity of the rationalist criterion. His point is that those who seek certainty misunderstand the nature and function of knowledge.

It so happens that Santayana introduced his own positive theory of knowing in juxtaposition to the rationalist criterion; discussion of the latter, abortive criterion led him to the development of his own views. But this is only a literary technique. Santayana thought that the presentation of his own view of knowledge would be more dramatic if it followed upon the collapse of the most widely respected alternative. This order of exposition naturally leads to the mistaken impression of continuity between the rationalist criterion and Santayana's own. It leaves the reader with the sense that Santayana grieves over the failure to achieve certainty and is pushed grudgingly to the acceptance of his own, less stringent and presumably also less desirable, criterion. But this is an altogether mistaken impression. Santayana considers the rationalist criterion of knowledge to be simply wrongheaded. He does not grieve over its failure and does not develop his own view as a miserable compromise. On the contrary, he thinks that the search for certainty and the subjectivistic turn that accompanied it have led thinkers away from sound common sense and therefore also away from sound philosophy. He explicitly proposes a return not only to the categories of the Greeks but also, and more importantly, to their starting point, which was to view human beings as natural organisms in a natural world.

The Development of His Thought

This explicit naturalism in Santayana's later works is supposed by some commentators to stand in sharp contrast with his earlier, more humanistic phase. These scholars divide Santayana's development into two main periods. The first begins with his *The Sense of Beauty* (1896) and continues through the five volumes of *The Life of Reason* (1905–06) until after Santayana's resignation from teaching in 1912. *Winds of Doctrine* (1913) is normally viewed as a work revealing the author's mind in transition. The second period begins with the publication of *Scepticism and Animal Faith* in 1923 and culminates in the four volumes of *The Realms of Being* (1927–40). *Dominations and Powers,* Santayana's last book published while he was still alive, shows signs of being a hybrid. But this is easily explained by the fact that it was put together during the last few years of Santayana's life from extensive notes, some of which had been written five decades earlier.

The view that Santayana underwent a major change in the middle of his philosophical career is made plausible by attention to the contrasts between the starting points, terminology, and central foci of the early and the later works. In the early writings, man commands the center of attention. Santayana attempts to deal with science, art, society, and religion as products of human creative activity. There is some evidence that he views nature as but the backdrop of the moral drama of human history. Frequently, the analyses appear subjectivistic; at any rate, they rarely transcend the intersubjective and unambiguously place man as a natural being in a natural world. The characterization of *The Life of Reason* as Santayana's version of Hegel's *Phenomenology* is not altogether unjust. The unwary reader is left with the impression that Santayana is tracing the history of the human spirit as it actualizes itself through its works.

By contrast, the later books view humans as but a species of animal in a natural world that far outstrips them in power. This world spins out of our cognitive grasp in the direction both of its most minute ingredients and of its momentous scope. The stress on human world-creation is altogether absent here. In its place, we are shown besieged in an uncaring, overwhelming environment. We struggle to find fulfillment or, in lieu of that, at least escape. The notion that reason can structure individual and social existence appears to be abandoned in favor of an ascetic spiritual life that yields, instead of domination over nature, only momentary release from frustration and disaster.

The frankly ontological emphasis of the later works appears also to separate them from the earlier studies of human faculties and functions. The differentiation of essence, matter, truth, and spirit seems alien to the thrust of those books, written while Santayana was still young, that focus on the analysis of symbolic structures found in religion and literature. The contrast is clear even when Santayana returns to the consideration of religion in *Platonism and the Spiritual Life* (1927) and *The Idea of Christ in the Gospels or God in Man* (1946). The analysis of religious life in these later books is itself cast in ontological terms. Much less attention is paid to the symbolic structures involved and much more to sorting out the ultimate categories in terms of which such activities can be understood.

Two Santayanas?

Commentators are justified in stressing these changes in Santayana's approach. They are evidently there and nothing is gained by minimizing them. If such a difference in approach and emphasis amounts to a change in literary persona, then it is reasonable to say that there are two Santayanas and not one.[10] But I do not think that changes in approach, emphasis, and terminology by themselves are adequate to establish ultimate differences in a thinker's commitments. The same fundamental points may be made in a scientific work as in a lyric poem; the language, the stress, the method will all differ then, but the message may well remain the same. If differences in approach and emphasis were ultimate, a tragedy and a comedy could not make the same substantive point. Yet we all know that this is clearly false: identity of thought easily survives the diversity of its media.

For the most part, Santayana's ideas remained unchanged through the years. I do not say this because I think steadfastness in one's convictions is necessarily a virtue. It may be, but it may also amount to an inability to learn. It just so happens that the basic vision of our philosopher remained essentially the same from the time of his graduate studies to the day of his death. We could call his views identical even if the relation of the earlier to the later were like the relation of the acorn to the oak. But in Santayana we cannot detect even such gradual organic growth. What we find, instead, is the same thought decked out in different garb, a little like the same actor playing different parts. In one case, the man on the stage may depict Shakespeare's Falstaff in full costume, with heavy makeup, affecting a British accent. A little later he is Willie Loman, an arch-American salesman baffled by the modern world. The actor is the same and through each play we can see the continuity of his ideas and his style. It would be absurd to think him different men and call him by different names just because he plays different roles on two successive nights.

Same Insight, Different Approaches

This analogy needs to be taken seriously. The reason for Santayana's early emphasis on man and human creations may well have been due to the fashion of the day. Santayana studied in Germany and read extensively in postcritical philosophy. Kant's Copernican revolution focused attention on the world-creative activity of man. Much subsequent philosophy in the nineteenth century began and ended with a study of man. History and the social world were thought to be the primary creatures of human activity. Even physical nature was conceived only through its role in the human world, or only as the receding horizon of alien necessity. Those raised under the influence of this tradition would naturally tend to cast their reflections in its terms; at any rate, in order to be understood and to be taken seriously it may have been necessary to start from this perspective.

Santayana's admiration of the Greeks itself became a natural ally of this approach. Aristotle thought that reason could and for the most part did shape human institutions and the good life. The insistence on the importance of reason could easily serve to focus attention on man as the bearer of this divine faculty. One could then readily forget Aristotle's *Physics* and his great metaphysical work *On the Soul,* and be so absorbed in the study of religion, art, and ethics as never to note the magnitude of the loss.

Viewed in this light, Santayana's later ontological emphasis may itself have been due to external influences. The twentieth century brought a sharp rejection of the humanistic idealism that dominated much of the intellectual life of the nineteenth. G. E. Moore, Bertrand Russell, and others with whom Santayana stayed in continued contact made crisp categories popular again. Instead of exploring the symbolic life of the mind, they insisted on starting from something that resembled common sense and on proceeding by the piecemeal analysis of concepts and the careful sharpening of distinctions. The realistic perspective that viewed the object of human knowledge as independent of the act of apprehending it became intellectually respectable again. G. E. Moore's "Refutation of Idealism" (1903)[11] had a profound impact on philosophers in the English-speaking world. This went hand in hand with new developments in logic that opened, to a thinker of Santayana's acuity, infinite realms of mind-independent objects. As a result at least partly of the growth of philosophical realism, even materialism became a conceivable alternative.

The Ontological Turn

This is the intellectual background against which Santayana's ontological turn, which was at once an explicit turn to realism and materialism, must be sketched. The philosophical environment naturally led him to recast his opinions in novel terms. The views themselves did not change appreciably; they came from the depths of his soul and could not easily be altered by external change. But the garb in which they were clothed, their whole external appearance, was redesigned. It is not that Santayana consciously went about constructing his thoughts to bring them in closer conformity with the fashion of the day. Intellectual changes do not occur in such a scheming or intentional way. Instead, the outer climate slowly penetrates the inner life. Unconsciously and without design, old ideas moult and soon begin wearing a new carapace.

His Steadfast View of the Human Condition

The most persuasive evidence that Santayana's thought remained essentially the same throughout the years is the steadiness of his vision of man. His view of religion, poetry, the arts, and even science as elements in the symbolic self-expression of the human race remained invariant. He was convinced from the first that consciousness is an impotent by-product of nature; this view is present in *The Life of Reason* no less than in the later works. He had the deepest moral certainty that values are relative to individuals and can be compared or measured against each other only in the private imagination.

If anything, Santayana's central ideas remained more steadfast than those of many major philosophers. Kant underwent a radical mutation from his precritical period to the philosophical volumes we normally associate with his name. Bertrand Russell notoriously changed his mind every few years. The comparison of Hume's philosophical writings with his work in history creates the impression of two altogether different minds. Plato himself passed through diverse phases traceable through the early, middle, and late dialogues. There is nothing resembling such philosophical upheavals or reversals in Santayana's work. The trappings, admittedly, change, but the central vision of our nature and possible fulfillment stands unaltered through a span of almost seventy years.

Interplay of His Experiences and Thought

There is another interesting way of viewing Santayana's philosophical development. We know relatively little about his private life, but even on this limited basis it is possible to correlate the changing emphases of his thought with changes in his own personal commitment. Santayana's stress on the power of reason in human life coincided not only with the afterglow left by the nineteenth century, but also with his own attempt to lead a relatively well-rounded and full human existence. The young professor at Harvard was a favorite of many. He had rich and talented friends, admiring students, and a safe, productive life that promised balanced fulfillments.

In retrospect, he claimed never to have been happy in his job or satisfied with his situation in Cambridge. At any rate, he gave up both voluntarily, at what he thought was his first opportunity to afford unemployed independence. World War I was a traumatic experience for Santayana, as it was for a whole generation of sensitive human beings. It dashed their hopes for international order; it shook their faith that reason ruled human behavior or at least shaped the outcome of events. Santayana suffered intensely during the war; although he was safe in England, he saw a world collapse around him. The letters he wrote to his friends during those years reflect his growing desperation and disillusionment. The later stress on the spiritual

life as a disintoxication from values may well have had its personal
origin in this experience.

Santayana's interest in the spiritual transcendence of the flux inten-
sified with his advancing years. Between the two wars he lived out of
a suitcase or two, traveling in Europe from city to city. He had obviously given up the attempt to lead the life of reason in a social setting: he was isolated in every way but intellectually. Even C. A.
Strong, his college friend and friendly philosophical rival, disappointed
him. His growing isolation led to virtual abandonment by the time
World War II began. It is evidently dangerous, and for scholars it is
thought an indiscretion, to relate their subject's views to changes in
his life. Yet beliefs are held by persons, and who those persons are and
what happens to them are in fact—though maybe not in an arid, conceptual way—related to their vicissitudes. Impersonal transcendence
must have seemed the only way to salvation for a man bereft of country
who had lost his faith in reason in the world. This does not mean that
he advocated the spiritual life as a manner of existence for others in
dissimilar circumstances. It is just that his own condition may have
made him see the point of such timeless union with essence in a way
he had never seen it before.

His Poetry

Some commentators bemoan the fact that Santayana essentially gave
up poetry when the flood of his philosophical books began to appear.
He himself thought that since English was not his native tongue, he
could never be a major poet in the language. This ultimate judgment
may well be right, but not for the reason he supposed. Santayana's
English is better than that of most who imbibed their language with
their mothers' milk. His mastery of the verbal medium is complete;
his writing is alive with rhythm and lit by metaphor. His poetry is less
than excellent because, I suspect, he was not by temperament a poet.

His poetry is traditional in form. For all the elegance of its well-
turned phrases, it is conceptually heavy. Poets must not think too
much or too systematically. Poetic form may be appropriate to convey
certain sorts of philosophical insight—Parmenides himself wrote down
his thoughts in verse. But such use of the medium makes for poor
poetry: the content overwhelms the form, reason crushes the imagination, and instead of a free creation we end up with the verbal equivalent of program music. It is to Santayana's immense credit as a poet

that he avoids this fate. The poems have an integrity all their own. yet it is evident that they carry freight; they have a message to convey and every word is meant to mean and not just to express or to evoke.

By natural bent Santayana was a thinker. He felt at home in the realm of ideas, of discursive thought eloquently expressed. His flirtation with poetry represents what I think was a process of content in search of adequate form. Poetry did not serve as an appropriate vehicle for what he wanted to say. Yet it was a natural candidate given the lilting rhythms of his heart. When form and content found each other at last in his work, his formal poetry dropped out. It was transmuted into the magnificent images of a richer prose, doing what only it could do: lighting the way so thought need never grope.

Catholic Atheist, Practical Man

Santayana was raised in the Roman Catholic Church. Yet he was an atheist. The combination of the two must have given rise to the apocryphal story according to which he believed that there is no God, and the Virgin Mary is His mother. In spite of his refusal to associate himself with an organized church, Santayana had an extraordinary sensitivity to the higher flights of the human imagination. He had a deep interest in such mystics as Saint John of the Cross, a native of Avila, the Santayana family's home. He had an easy and vibrant sympathy with the subtlest emotions of the religious life. And his interpretation of the Nicene Creed in the terms of his own philosophy is one of the most remarkable translations of Christian theology into secular wisdom. [12]

The overall impression one may get of this complex and secretive person is that of a flight of mind dragging the senses, the emotions, and the body reluctantly with it. Yet this image is superficial. Santayana himself attacked philosophies that were mere free-floating ideas without honest attachment to the facts. And as an individual, Santayana showed rare judgment and practical sense. His letter to Cory when the younger man was inflicted with the wages of indiscriminate lust is a masterpiece of wisdom and compassion. [13] He was no less wise and circumspect in handling difficult human relations in C. A. Strong's unhappy family. Even the way in which he dealt with financial matters, including Cory's virtually total fiscal reliance on him, shows considerable common sense and knowledge of human nature.

Santayana was emphatically not an impractical philosopher with a beautiful mind. He may have viewed the world as his host, but he was not a shy or reluctant guest. He was, and hoped to be, a person of good sense and good taste. He intended to have his philosophy reflect these traits. It is for this reason, if for no other, that we must take his thought seriously. A world that suffers from the lack of both can afford to reject the offer of neither.

Chapter Two
Skepticism as Mental Exercise
The Plausibility of Universal Skepticism

Some philosophers maintain that wholesale skepticism is not an intelligible position or attitude. To be dubious about the truth of any given judgment or the validity of any one perception presupposes, they say, that we know what it would be like for a judgment to be true or for a perception to reveal the world. Skeptical doubts make sense only by contrast with knowledge and certainty; if we had no knowledge, it would be senseless, nay impossible, to doubt. In this light, knowledge is sometimes likened to money and error to the work of the counterfeiter. There could be no counterfeits, it is urged, if there were no money that is good and legal tender. Similarly, the very admission that error can occur or that doubt is legitimate is supposed to adumbrate a broad structure of valid cognitions.

This approach has a warm glow of plausibility. We all tend to believe that knowledge is possible; we all experience levels of conviction which, we think, could not be more intense. We recognize cases where doubt is appropriate by the sharp contrast they exhibit with instances in which our knowledge seems secure. Why not reject, then, the very possibility of systematic doubt as but an idle invention of armchair philosophy?

The most important reason for taking the possibility of large-scale doubt seriously is that it can assault us in the form of a vigorously and emotionally lived experience. For many of us, skepticism is a natural attendant of adolescent rebellion. In the struggle to achieve autonomy in beliefs and life, young people naturally come to question the thoughts and habits their parents imposed on them in their early years. Frequently the rebellion is religious and moral: favorite dogmas are challenged, hitherto authoritative values lose their force or their self-evidence. The impact on the behavior of the child may be profound but it is insignificant by comparison with the havoc it wreaks in the inner life. There, ideas come to move in a flux without stability and direction, like waves in the middle of the ocean.

Moreover, an absolute skepticism is not at all inconceivable. Once we find that a favorite opinion turns out to be false, we can readily think the same of *any* idea. And if any idea may be false, there is nothing to stop us from fearing that they all are. To be sure, this implies that we judge our ideas by a standard—and a high one at that. But that does not require that we *know* the standard, only that we hold it, albeit experimentally. If asked whether this is the right standard or not, it is always possible to answer that we do not know. This does not cheapen the skeptical stance. On the contrary, it carries it to its logical extreme. For then we do not even claim to know that we cannot know; we say only that we know not whether we know or not.

Skeptics through the ages have used a variety of images to make universal skepticism plausible or at least easy to conceive. Descartes proposed the possibility of a malevolent demon intent on deceiving us. Others suggested that perhaps all of life is but an elaborate dream. It would be a mistake to take such an image as more than just that: it is an aid to the imagination in conceiving what might at first seem unlikely or alien. But once we move inside the analogy of the whole world existing only in a dream, instead of carping at its incidental features, we find that the idea has a logic and plausibility all its own. For we frequently dream worlds that neither were nor can ever be, but we know the sharp deception only because we awake. It is only by comparison with the world we know once we awake that the world we dreamt is branded as a dream.

But sometimes our dreams are too good to be true. The mind cannot believe that all could go so well, attempts to wake itself, and dreams that it succeeds. We then dream that we wake up and compare the world we dreamt with what we now dream is real life. In this way, the entire contrast between dream and waking is transposed into our dreams and "reality" turns out to be our latest fantasy.

Skepticism in Modern Philosophy

Philosophers from Descartes on have been intensely conscious of the possibility of skepticism. It is not that there had been no skeptics before the modern age. It is just that such early persons of doubt were considered heretics to be dealt with or oddities to deride. In modern philosophy, by contrast, skepticism became an alternative to reckon with, a permanent threat one needed to avoid. There was a special reason for this keen consciousness of the danger to our edifice of knowledge.

The ancients were well aware of the contradictions and unreliabilities of human perception. New discoveries in science from the seventeenth century on, however, appeared to add poignancy to the suspicion of the defectiveness of our senses. Scientists concluded early that the physical world could not be anything like the world we perceive. There seemed to them to be adequate evidence to believe that the world was a single system of particles moving in space. Such atoms were thought to have movement and location, extension, shape and mass, viz. all the properties necessary to explain their behavior singly or attached to one another in the form of physical objects. These features of the ultimate units of existence were designated "primary qualities." They were believed to be the only objective properties of real things. This immediately relegated the bulk of the sensory characteristics of physical objects to the level of the merely subjective. The color, taste, sound, even the feel of the external world were thus thought to be inaccurate, if taken as representations of reality. The redness of the stove could well serve as a useful reminder to us that it is not to be touched; but in reality there was no redness there, only a mass of whirling molecules. The redness was the lyrical contribution of the mind, useful perhaps but literally false.

This supposed revelation of physics concerning the cognitive inadequacy of our senses came as a major blow to both science and philosophy. For physics itself depended for its results on the assumption that the senses gave reliable knowledge; yet the knowledge they gave, when systematized in the body of physics, brought disrepute to the "secondary qualities" which constitute the bulk of sensory life. Those who wanted to pull the sting of science, such as the empiricist Bishop George Berkeley, argued that secondary qualities and primary qualities were inseparable. For this reason, they thought, whatever strictures are appropriate against secondaries also count against the primaries. Conversely, whatever cognitive value primary qualities may have is shared by the secondaries. Berkeley, for one, clearly thought that this argument tended to reestablish the credibility of the senses, for if the primary qualities revealed reality, so did the secondaries. But the matter could as readily turn out the other way, leading to the conclusion that if the secondary qualities are unreliable indicators of the real properties of objects, so are the primaries.

The distinction between the real properties of physical objects and their relational properties, viz. those which are due at least in part to our subjective contribution to them, introduced a sharp line between matter and mind, between the subject and objective reality. Secondary qualities were supposed to exist only for consciousness, they had their being only "in" the mind. Extra-mental reality, by contrast, soon appeared as but the distant original that our senses attempted but failed to reduplicate. Since we could get to reality only by means of our own ideas, we could never be altogether sure that our perceptions were accurate. It was not long before sharp and reckless minds detected that, on the basis of these assumptions, there would always be doubt not only about the properties but also about the existence of external, physical objects.

Skepticism with regard to the senses and the external world was, then, closely connected with the subjective turn in modern philosophy. The attempt to relieve our doubts about perception, the search for certainty led directly to the inner world. If sure truth was to be found anywhere, it was in the immediacies of consciousness. If we could not be certain about the existence or nature of the external world, perhaps we could be sure at least about our ideas of it. Thus Descartes himself felt that we can gain no secure footing for the edifice of knowledge until we discover that some, at least, of our ideas are indubitable. I may doubt the existence of anything in particular, but it makes no sense at all to doubt that I doubt. It may well be, later empiricists maintained, that the object I seem to see is not really red, but there can be no doubt that there is a red patch or flash present to my consciousness. In this way, private, subjective conscious life came to supply the certainty that escaped us in the external world. Even when Kant and others attempted a reconstruction of philosophy, it was typically out of such subjective elements that reality was to be remade.

Santayana on Skepticism

Santayana was deeply attracted to the objectivistic and naturalistic starting point of the Greeks. The entire sceptical and subjectivist turn appeared to him to have been an unfortunate incident in the history of Western thought. There is reason to believe that he wished to bypass and disregard the entire skeptical tradition. Yet that was impossible for at least two reasons. He himself was a thoroughly modern man, by nature searching, suspicious, skeptical. He had the gravest doubts about the universality of values, the literal adequacy of knowledge, the ultimate prospects of man in the world. Moreover, he knew that he had to come to grips with the skeptical and subjectivistic reductions of human experience. A philosophy that failed to speak to these issues could have no plausibility to the modern mind. For these reasons and perhaps for others as well, all unstated by him, he decided to take skepticism head on.

In *Scepticism and Animal Faith* Santayana attacked the modern skeptic with characteristically clever strategy.[1] Instead of engaging in the futile attempt of presenting arguments against him, Santayana joins his antagonist to see where the full development of the skeptical position might lead. His studies in the history of philosophy convinced him that skeptical reductions were never fully and consistently carried out. Instead, doubt would be pursued no further than was necessary to impugn rival dogmas and to arrive at one's own favorite conclusion. For once, Santayana decided, doubt should be carried to its final limits to see where it leaves us. For once, the skeptical eye should not blink when it comes to dogmas that seem attractive or inevitable. If the relentless search for certainty reduces us to silence, we shall simply have to bear the consequences; if some surprising belief escapes its destructive force, we shall have to start our philosophical reconstruction from that one firm fact.

Is there anything we must believe? The first casualties of skepticism come from among the optional beliefs of religion. For most of us it takes no special effort to disbelieve in God or in immortality. Some of the dogmas of religion are difficult enough to understand; when we understand them they are difficult to believe. Rejection of them liberates the mind by simplifying our view of the structure of existence. We can then be hard-headed and believe only what we see. Such tough-minded empiricism eliminates not only belief in God. It also blots out the future, which is the realm of what is yet to be, the as-yet unformed and thus the unknowable. And, perhaps not altogether surprisingly, the future and the past are in the same boat. Although the past is fully formed and looms unchangeably behind us, it also is inaccessible to the senses. We only remember it, and memories are notoriously deceiving.

Our Senses and Memories Can Deceive

That memories deceive is well known to everyone from personal experience. The problem is that rememberings and mis-rememberings are somehow all alike: there is no internal mark by which we could distinguish the false from the true. Memories that turn out to be false initially carry the same compulsive force as those we find, by corroboration, to be true. And even those we think true can be verified only by reference to other memories that we or others have: direct verification is impossible.

It is not difficult to suppose that the entire edifice of our beliefs about the past is an imaginative creation. The distant past of geologic ages and early human history is revealed to us only by extensive interpretation and tenuous inferences from present data; nothing is simpler than to think that the resulting stories are fanciful, fictionalized accounts. Our own history is ill-remembered. Any supporting documents, such as birth certificates, themselves are worthless as evidence unless we entertain supervenient beliefs that they were authentically produced and actually represent events that once took place. It is not altogether beyond the human imagination to conceive that we were created but a minute ago with all the "memories" we have. If so, everything we tend to, or are tempted to, believe about events that happened months or years ago, would in fact be utterly and irremediably false. Yet they would hang together in a single edifice, pretending to corroborate one another, like the lies of a gang of thieves.

If we can doubt the reality of the future and of the past, can we not doubt the veracity of the senses? Here, once again, the problem is not that the senses occasionally mislead. It is rather that instances of perception and misperception are internally indistinguishable. From the standpoint of how they are experienced, seeing a gnu at the zoo and seeing a pink snake at the bar are no different: each animal is as convincingly present as the other. It is only in retrospect that we declare one to have been an illusion and cleverly assign the cause to drunkenness. But we have already seen that to do so in retrospect involves the unreasonable assumption of the veracity of memory. And, in any case, is it unreasonable to suppose that we see reality only when drunk? Even if this seems implausible to the sober mind, it is enough to reveal that the contrary view is itself nothing but belief, corroborated perhaps, but to some measure dubious.

The fact that no sense perception has the internal mark of truth is further demonstrated by the frequent conflict of equally compelling sense experiences. A pail of lukewarm water will seem hot to the right hand recently removed from contact with a block of ice, while it seems cold to the left that has just worked around a steaming crab pot.

Which hand shall we believe? Each is equally insistent that *its* message is correct and we cannot decide by reference to where the hands had been, because our memory is unreliable. And the famous stick thrust in water really looks bent, even though the hand exploring it finds it straight. Shall we trust our eyes or our hands? There is nothing in either perception that would reveal it as counterfeit. We simply decide to trust one over the other because we think that the bulk of the evidence supports it. But the evidence itself consists of memories and sense perceptions, and to view any sensory belief as corroborated by others is already to assume that those others are true or confirmed. If the evidence itself is in need of confirmation, it cannot serve to render anything secure.

If this is inadequate to cast doubt on the operation of the senses, we can take skepticism a step further. The reason why we think that perceptions reveal reality is that their objects appear to have compelling presence independent of our will. But are such objects in fact present in sense perception? When I perceive a glittering diamond, what is the immediate object of my sensory activities? I do not *see* that it is a diamond, I only think that because it is offered for sale as such. What I see is a flash of light, the colors of the rainbow, and a certain size and shape. The flash and the colors and the visual extension do not amount to a physical object. Physical objects are three-dimensional occupants of space with a life history that stretches through a measurable time. The immediately presented flash, the colors, the shape stand as but indications that there may well be something there: the permanence, the past and the future of this putative object, however, are only inferred. It involves a bold assumption for me to say that this flashy something in front of me now is not merely the sort of momentary blaze jewelers know how to create, which fades as soon as I pay and leave the store.

The affair is even more complicated with "thick," nontransparent objects such as tables and chairs and barrels of malt liquor. For what I see of them immediately is but a portion of what I presume to be their surface. Yet physical objects are supposed to have not only fronts, but backs and insides as well. When I see the front, I only believe that there is a back. And if I were to turn to check this as quickly as I could, I would simply be faced with another front whose back (my previous front) I can now only recall. The point of this entire exercise is to accomplish what painters routinely do, viz. to separate the actually present visual elements from what we, because of our perceptual habits, naturally believe. These beliefs may or may not be valid; the important thing is that they are always open to doubt.

Doubts about the Self

These arguments were common coin by the time Santayana came to consider them. His contribution to the history of skepticism is the forceful way he went beyond them. He saw that some of the same considerations that cast doubt on the veracity of senses and memory also damage the case of our presumed knowledge of the self and of change in general. David Hume had already noted that even the most careful introspection failed to reveal the presence of any being properly called a "self." A self would have to be an enduring existent. As such, its history would have to be remembered and was hence a matter of presumption. All we could catch of it were the individual feelings and ideas that floated to the surface of consciousness at any given time. That these immediate presentations constituted a system stretching through time was an agreeable belief and no more.

The internal landscape and the pictorial world of our extended senses present us with the same material: immediately apprehended qualities of a myriad sorts. Just as there is no certainty about the world, so there is no possibility of really knowing the self. The most we can hope for is belief tenuously extrapolated from what is immediately present. And no such belief can meet the rigorous standards of the skeptic: it is always possible that what we believe is in fact untrue.

Can we not rest in Descartes's certainty that, even though I can doubt many things, I can never doubt that I am doubting? Santayana's devastating answer is that the *I* that doubts, an active, rational being, is never to be found among the objects of our consciousness. If there is such a being, it is not one with which we are directly acquainted; hence its existence, presence, and operations constitute matters of fallible belief. Even the assertion that there is doubt*ing,* or any other activity of the *I,* presupposes a risky inference from the present to the absent. For mental activities appear in consciousness only through their products, the ideas and feelings we experience. That there are purposive activities underlying and perhaps causing these ideas is a matter not of immediate certainty but of conjecture or hypothesis. Doubt is impossible only about the immediate object that floats before the mind—in Descartes's case, the directly encountered doubt. If we want certainty, we can have neither the I nor its activity in doubting, only the doubt lived or suffered through. In asserting that this doubt is mine or that it is an activity in which I engage, I go beyond the limits of certainty to what I cannot know for sure, but hope I have enough reason to believe.

Doubts about Change

The immediate object of consciousness appears almost always to be in a process of change. If we can have absolute certainty about this datum, can we not know its properties as well? Such immediate grasp or intuition of change, of relatedness to the past and future, could serve as the bedrock on which knowledge of causal and other temporal relations might be built. In fact, something like this is the center of the antiskeptical strategy of Santayana's contemporaries, Whitehead and Hartshorne. In response to this challenge, Santayana takes the last, striking step in the development of his skepticism.

He begins by noting that real change can never be immediately presented. Such alteration is not the property of any one datum of consciousness; it is the relation that obtains between successive data. A single moment of awareness can present us only with a picture of change, such as the experience of the movement of long fingernails down my back. The feeling is one of luscious change, it is not, *at any one moment* when I enjoy it, a changing feeling. To be sure, it may change over even a short time, but at any given time it is changelessly just what it is. Change in consciousness occurs when a new, even if not too dissimilar, datum takes the place of a previous one. Alteration, then, requires the succession that takes place from one moment to another: it is not a feature of any one object of consciousness, but the exchange of features or properties over a stretch of time.

This means that change is never directly apprehended. What we immediately grasp is some stable datum, such as the cast of a dark and cloudy sky, followed by another, say, the brilliance of lightning. Neither datum is a change; change occurs *from* the former *to* the latter and is, therefore, never presented in a single moment. Absolute certainty about it thus escapes us. At the earlier moment, the change has not yet taken place. At the later moment, what we perceived a second before is but a memory. We only *believe* that there was such a prior moment: for all we *know,* any sense of a past is an illusion and this flash of lightning is all of reality.

What can we know with certainty? Only what is transparently be-

fore the mind. And even that can be known only at the time and for
the duration of its presence. There is, of course, nothing we can know
or say *about* such immediate objects. The formulation of judgments
this would involve requires change in the form of the action of the
mind as it unites subject and predicate. All we can do is to take in the
object, to absorb and to contemplate it as a whole. Even this language
is deceptive, for it suggests activity and a distinction between subject
and object, neither of which is ever directly presented. In the state to
which the search for certainty reduces us, there is nothing but the
manifest object which appears.

Solipsism

The outcome of a rigorously executed skeptical program is, thus,
what Santayana calls "solipsism of the present moment."[2] By this he
means that there is no certainty except in the speechless absorption in
whatever object may float before the mind. "Solipsism" has traditionally been the name of the exotic philosophical view that one's own self
is the only real existent. Given this standard meaning, Santayana's designation of the outcome of skepticism as solipsism of the present moment is doubly inappropriate. First, certainty for him is emphatically
not about self, but about impersonal objects given in consciousness.
Since *ipse* means "self" and *datum* means "given" in Latin, Santayana's
view should be called sol-datism of the present moment. Second, solipsism maintains that there is at least something that exists, namely a
self. Santayana, on the other hand, thinks that he is not in a position
at this stage to assert the existence of anything. In fact, his analysis of
the consequences of skepticism leaves him with changeless data, the
existence of which he explicitly denies.

Santayana on Existence

It may seem odd to say that something I immediately confront
and whose presence is a silent certainty, nevertheless does not exist.
Yet Santayana's concept of existence, which is the ground of this
claim, is not far removed from our ordinary notion. When we say that
something exists, we mean at least that it can be found as an item
separate from others, that it endures for a while, and that it can do a
variety of things to affect its neighbors. This is the notion of existence
we have in mind when we say that the Atlantic Ocean exists but

Socrates does not any more, that snakes exist but the square root of seven never did.

Santayana refines this common idea of existence and uses it with far greater consistency than the average person. He employs the word "existence" to designate "such being as is in flux, determined by external relations and jostled by irrelevant events."[5] He does not deny that the data of consciousness are real in some sense of that ambiguous term. But not everything real qualifies as an existent. To exist is to engage in activities and by means of them to be related to other objects. The activities are diverse and the objects variable; change and happenstance permeate existence to the core. And the relations among existing things are not like those that obtain between the interconnected members of a harmonious system. On the contrary, each existing unit is buffeted by the alien force of innumerable others, each stands outside of and only contingently related to all the rest.

The reason Santayana asserts that nothing given exists and that no existing object is ever directly apprehended by the mind is twofold. The first is the conclusion he reaches at the end of his skeptical analysis, that each object of consciousness is by itself unchanging. The second is the observation that such changeless objects constitute integral unities with inseparable parts. As a result, each datum is a self-contained world whose parts are internally related to—which is to say, immutably necessary for—the whole. Since no existence has these features, nothing of which we are immediately aware can be an agent in the flux of nature.

Invincible Skepticism

The skeptical reduction leaves us with certainty only about data. Knowledge of existence is shown to be impossible. Inquiry, judgment, and communication are futile or unreliable. Past and future become perspectives incorporated in the present datum. Self, change, and action are reduced to images of themselves without power or outcome. The work of thought itself is transformed into appearance, and all that is left is passive, speechless, thoughtless absorption in the moment.

On its own grounds, skepticism is invincible; does this not show the impotence of the human intellect? Perhaps the only legitimate function of philosophy is to discover the horrendous illusion of thinking we can know, so that we may with good conscience abandon the

futile quest. In its place, we could devote our lives to feeling, blind
action, or aesthetic enjoyment of the immediate, though no consistent
skeptic could ever find reasons for recommending this. A less sensible
philosopher than Santayana might well have ended his reflections on
this note. But Santayana, though frequently accused of having an impractical bent, actually has a robust sense of reality. He notes that,
even in the skeptic, doubt does not amount to disbelief: while the
intellect raises artful objections to everything, the business of life mer-
rily proceeds. Optional doubts make no dent in the structure of compulsory belief expressed in our actions: in his victory, the skeptic
succeeds only in rendering his thought irrelevant to his life.

There is indeed a conclusion other than the worthlessness of reason
that may be drawn from the invincibility of the skeptic. If we find that
knowledge cannot be achieved, the standard we set for it may well be
too severe. Standards must bear a sensible relation to capacity; it would
be absurd to say that humans cannot jump because they never clear the
bar at fifty feet. To be sure, some norms are temptingly simple or seem
naturally right. But this must not blind us to the need to assess criteria, as well; none is self-justifying or uncriticizably true.

The skeptic wins by setting standards that cannot be met. His criterion of knowledge is absolute certainty, which is much more difficult
to achieve than the feeling of assurance that comes naturally to the
gullible man. Such certainty has traditionally been thought possible
only about self-evident and necessary truths. The former were supposed
to shine by their own light: not assenting to them was tantamount to
not understanding them. Descartes's claims that I cannot doubt that I
doubt and that since I think I exist, are examples of such presumably
self-justifying verities. The latter were judgments whose falsity was
unthinkable because it would involve a self-contradiction. That bachelors are unmarried is an instance of this sort of truth, since its denial,
that some bachelors at least are married people, is senseless because of
its inconsistency.

A steadfast skeptic can readily show that certainty in these forms is
unattainable, if for no other reason at least because they require the
formulation of judgments. Such activity presupposes short term or immediate memory, which is always fallible. The skeptic then announces
the failure of human reason, but without abandoning his exacting,
rationalistic standard of knowledge. Paradoxically, his skeptical critique never extends to his own criteria. As a result, he remains a rationalist, albeit a frustrated one.

The Skeptic's Standard Too High

Santayana's conclusion is that the rationalist criterion of knowledge, with its demand for certainty, in unrealistically high. The problem is not that human reason fails to come up to the ideal it should reach, but that the skeptic's ideal fails to measure adequately the achievement of reason. The solution is not to abandon the search for understanding, but to reject the wrongheaded criterion.

There is yet another way to view the skeptic's rationalist program. It is an attempt to emancipate the mind from all physical concerns. Everyone knows that certainty in practical matters is impossible and that the senses provide rich but fallible information. The rationalist begins by disregarding practical life and the cognitive apparatus of the body, to see what the mind can do on its own. His standard is set without reference to the power and limits of embodied intellect: it is designed to take the measure of a divinely potent disembodied mind. The result is a loss of seriousness through the loss of relevance. The skeptical reduction becomes a game, an exercise to limber mental muscles, instead of the humane inquiry it set out to be.

Santayana does not deny that the mind is capable of acting as though it were disembodied. In what he calls "the spiritual life," consciousness completely transcends the cares of animal existence by exclusive attention to the immediate. But the spiritual life is aesthetic, not intellectual: it yields joy in whatever is presented, not an understanding of existence or a grasp of truths about the world. Such free play of the mind is perfectly all right, so long as it is recognized for what it is— the momentary perfection of a dependent organ—and not confused with the earnest labor of rational inquiry. The notion of the spiritual life can well be a part of one's philosophy, but the rest of one's thought must deal with the concerns that beset mind in its physical station. The skeptic wrongly supposes that the standards of consciousness in its purity have any application to its work in the real world. The mind is not legislator of the world, only a small light in the pervasive dark.

The Value of Skepticism

A questioning attitude. Santayana's merciless application of doubt succeeds in discrediting both wholesale skepticism and the rationalist criterion of knowledge that underlies it. But in addition to this negative outcome, the skeptical reduction also affords him three

critically important positive results. The first is a cast of mind particularly well suited to the pursuit of philosophical inquiry. Universal
doubt enables Santayana to develop a keen sense for the tenuousness of
all human beliefs. In the very process of showing the inadequacy of
wholesale skepticism, he appears to have learned the value of suspicion
about individual ideas. His habit of questioning the accepted and looking for equally valid alternatives is present throughout his work,
though nowhere more clearly than in his assessment of morality. Distance if not disillusionment characterizes his view of human values,
and his relation to the political and philosophical fashions of his day is
always skeptical. His steely, disintegrative vision enables him to present a picture of human life as it might appear viewed through the
wrong end of binoculars. His tendency to question and examine renders his thought sophisticated and, in spite of his scholastic terminology, thoroughly modern.

    The discovery of essence.   The second positive result of the
skeptical reduction is the discovery of essences. His idea of essence is
perhaps the greatest stumbling block to the appreciation of Santayana's
philosophy. Yet the idea is simple and liberating. The key to understanding it is to remember that Santayana restricts the notion of existence to externally related objects in the changing physical world. The
immediate data of consciousness are clearly not such objects: each is
all-encompassing in its presence, internally related to its elements, and
unchanging. They are, therefore, not existences, yet they are patently
real. It is crucial that we not think of them as full-bodied or even
shadowy physical things, though some of them are forms physical objects may assume and minds may contemplate. The charge that Santayana's world is vastly overpopulated because of all these essences,
rests on the mistake of not keeping this in mind. No one needs to be
concerned that these essences may become a drain on our resources.

    Santayana indicates that there are a number of ways in which we can
arrive at the notion of essence. Mathematicians and logicians, reflecting on their explorations, may come to see that they deal with an
infinite realm of nonexistent forms. Artists may isolate pure sensuous
structures such as colors, sounds, or shapes unconnected to any actual
thing. Mystics and those given to more intellectual modes of contemplation may recognize the objects in which they are absorbed as eternal
beings enjoying their own form of reality. But no avenue to essence is
as readily accessible as the skeptical reduction. And a special advantage

of that approach is that it makes the self-standing reality of essences perfectly obvious.

We noted earlier that the immediate datum of consciousness is not physical. But it is not mental either. To be mental, it would have to be the act of consciousness to which data appear. Such a living act is necessary if any essence is to be bathed in the light of attention, but it is never presented as a part of the object beheld. Essences are not, intrinsically, even properties and relations of physical things or data of awareness. They may well be used as such when the physical world or consciousness adopts them for a while, but in their inner nature they are neutral between matter and mind.

Essences, then, are the qualities, structures, and relations that make existence possible. They are the garbs the world wears, the features, simple and complex, of embodied reality. They are also the themes of human thought and animal feeling, the objects of "intuition," which is Santayana's word for consciousness. But they are much more than this, as well, because indefinitely many essences can or will never be embodied or beheld. Essences constitute an infinite "continuum of discrete forms"[4]; their totality is what Santayana calls "the realm of essence." Yet "realm" is, once again, not to be interpreted as an actual cosmos or existing world, only a sum of real but nonexistent qualities and relations.

There are an infinite number of essences, yet they occupy as little space as the hope for a better harvest. They cannot be found the way snakes can under rocks because, intrinsically, they have no location in physical space. They also have no native place in the flux of time. Santayana is careful to distinguish between the everlasting, which endures from the beginning to the end of time, and the eternal which, though ever accessible to what exists in time, itself never inhabits it.[5] Essences are eternal in this sense, and since they do not undergo change, they are indestructible. This sounds like a good thing, but it is counterbalanced by the fact that, being in neither time nor space, they lack all causal power. They are passively available to give form to the world and content to our thoughts, but if this possibility is to be actualized, the action must come from the side of existing beings.

The philosophy of animal faith. The third positive outcome of Santayana's resolute skepticism is a profoundly new direction for his philosophy. The rationalist criterion of knowledge has proved itself bankrupt. A subjectivist starting point has typically been associated with the modern search for certainty: the natural assumption of think-ers engaged in the quest has been that initial or bedrock assurance is not to be found apart from the internal states of the inquirer. This subjectivism falls with the unreasonably demanding standard of knowl-edge. The double collapse sets Santayana free to find a new starting point and to formulate a new criterion. His guide in doing so is the desire to remedy the ultimate irrelevance to which skepticism leads; he wants a philosophy firmly rooted in the activities of life. If he were not the heir of Descartes and Hume, Santayana could simply begin with an account of the world and man's place in it. But the modern preoc-cupation with method and knowledge makes such a classical beginning impossible. Although his primary interest focuses on what there is, Santayana must first deal with how and what we can know of it.

This determines the shape of Santayana's own philosophy. He takes as his primary fact the activity of human beings in the natural world. Although this environment is vast and sometimes treacherous, we ap-proach it with "animal faith," an unreflective confidence in its basic structures. For a philosophy to have relevance to life, it must be a discernment and critical articulation of the details of this trust. Phi-losophy is the systematic discovery of the tenets of animal faith.

Chapter Three
An Honest Philosophy of Action
Method in the Philosophy of Animal Faith

To discover the tenets of animal faith, we must examine the interaction between human organism and environment. In the thick of such give and take we embody our deepest convictions about the world and ourselves. That is the plan I shall follow in this chapter although, surprisingly, it is not Santayana's procedure. He clearly announces that the philosophy of animal faith represents a radical break with the rationalist criterion of knowledge, yet he is reluctant to leave the skeptic mired in his solipsism of the present moment and simply start anew. Instead, he sets out to show how attention to what we as animals instinctively believe impels us to add belief after belief to the cognitive austerity of the skeptic.

Santayana's manner of proceeding has the advantage of symmetry: while skepticism gradually destroys beliefs, animal faith little by little restores them. It also makes for a neat continuity that displays the idea of animal faith as the insight that rescues the skeptic from a troublesome and fruitless position. But there are disadvantages, as well. The stress on continuity tends to distract attention from the fact that the philosophy of animal faith is a new initiative whose standard of knowledge is an alternative to the skeptic's. Consequently, in attempting to rescue the skeptic by showing all we know, Santayana appears to leave himself open to criticism in terms of the skeptic's criterion. And the gradual extrication from solipsism of the present moment may create the mistaken impression that the proper starting point of Santayana's own philosophy is the internal condition of the subject or the intuition of essence.[1]

In fact, of course, nothing could be farther from the truth. The philosophical method that focuses on the explication of animal beliefs takes human action as the given; the existence of mind is not among its first tenets. Santayana's deliberate starting point is clearly objective; by his own admission, it is much closer to Aristotle's than to Descartes's. Another way to make this point is to stress that rejecting the skeptical enterprise is tantamount to surrendering presuppositionless epistemology. There can be no sound standards in the theory of knowledge without prior commitments in metaphysics, without the initially uncritical assumption of the reality of human action.

Santayana's exposition in *Scepticism and Animal Faith* tends to obscure this resolute break with modern, subjectivist tradition. It tends also to underplay his kinship with such pragmatists as Dewey. Finally, it makes it unnecessarily difficult to display the proper order and strength of the beliefs implicated in action. We will do better to deal with animal faith directly and leave all references to the skeptical reduction behind.

Faith and Action

When Santayana speaks of animal "faith," he does not intend to evoke any religious or spiritualistic connotations. His occasional use of the phrase "empirical confidence" and his accounts of what he has in mind make it perfectly clear that "faith" refers simply to the attitude of unreflecting trust we all display towards certain features of the natural world. This faith exists unarticulated below the level of consciousness. We can marshal no arguments for it, because the very enterprise of offering evidence presupposes it and would be impossible in its absence. Fortunately, since it is not an intellectual conviction, it needs no propositional proof; Santayana says that the evident success of acting on it is enough to establish it as a permanent disposition.

We must be careful to avoid a possible misunderstanding here. To say that we *act on* the beliefs of animal faith might misleadingly suggest that we are aware of them; with such beliefs it is perhaps better to say that we *act them out.* For we do, for example, sometimes *act out* our anger without being aware that we are mad. And our behavior constantly embodies laws of physics and psychology, even though we may be totally ignorant of the existence or the nature of these laws. The philosopher's job is to discern what beliefs our actions reveal, that is, what convictions would fill our minds if the principles governing our conduct were adequately reflected there. This requires sensitivity and good sense, and the results are subject to correction by anyone of keener vision.

When Santayana speaks of identifying the beliefs implicated in action, he does not think of action in any technical philosophical sense. Although philosophers sometimes distinguish conscious and perhaps purposive action from mere behavior, this is not a useful contrast for understanding his thought. By "action" he means the primarily physical but adaptive and sometimes intelligent interplay of the individual with his or her environment. Action in this sense is an observable feature of the world; the distinction between conscious action and "mere" behavior is part of a theoretical embellishment on what we see. In his claims about the central importance of the human psyche and the physical impotence of consciousness, Santayana himself hazards some theories. But they, too, are subsequent to the primordial sense of "action" with which he begins.

What sorts of beliefs can we hope to find implicated in our ordinary actions? Beliefs that reflect individual peculiarities of our situation can have little philosophical significance. We must, therefore, look for shared commitments, for principles naturally embodied in the activity of all agents. To achieve such universality, the beliefs cannot be very specific: not only does my thought "There is a squirrel in the yard" fail to be a tenet of animal faith, so does the more general idea "There are squirrels." Animal beliefs can come only from among notions expressing the most general features of the world and of ourselves as we encounter it. But not even all of these will qualify: some, such as the universal logical property of any pair of objects a and b, that if a implies b, then we never get a without b, are not of any direct significance to action. In looking for what the active animal believes, we are not trying to determine what it would hold if it thought long and carefully about its situation. For this reason, if for no other, the tenets of animal faith are not identical with even the most fundamental scientific laws: they are simpler, more schematic, and more indeterminate than anything science would find satisfactory. Animal faith is the relatively vague but operationally adequate common sense of the human race.

A Threatening Encounter

Let us take as our paradigm of action my encounter with a large, unpleasant man downtown. The streets are empty and he moves toward me in a threatening way. I prepare to run but want to show no fear. I wonder if a quick kick would distract him enough to let me get away. My fear is that he runs faster, that he will strike first, that he may hardly feel my kick.

My explicit beliefs in this situation are plain enough. The tacit commitments of animal faith underlie these beliefs and make them possible. First and foremost, animal action presumes the independent existence of a world. The man I meet is clearly not myself and downtown exists without the aid of any minds. They are parts of a reality I did not create and do not sustain; they are objects with independent histories without which there could be no chance encounters.

Realism

I feel embarrassed at having to make such an obvious point. But what common sense unhesitatingly affirms, philosophers have spent hundreds of years denying. Realism is the view that the world exists independently of perception, conception, and any other activity of consciousness, and in modern philosophy it has been a contested if not downright unpopular position. Of course, the cleverest thinkers made the mind-dependence of the world a subtle and elusive affair. Bishop George Berkeley, for example, argued that all of perceivable reality was sustained by the imperceptible consciousness of God. This belief enabled him to cleave to his favored but implausible view of the all-pervasive primacy of mind without the absurdity of denying the facts of daily experience. Kant's arcane theory of the world-creative activity of consciousness behind the scenes, which made it possible for him to claim that physical objects were independent of us in ordinary life and mind-generated only on a deeper, transcendental analysis, was designed to accomplish the same end. Santayana has little patience with such artful metaphysical theorizing because its transparent purpose is to discredit in thought what we rely on in practice.

Idealistic philosophers first accept the deliverances of common sense and then, by some deft moves of high theory, deny them. If the ideas of the ordinary person were merely one set of beliefs among alternatives, philosophers could challenge and perhaps even replace them. But they are much more: as tenets of animal faith, the entire practice of the race supports them. Even idealists embrace them through their actions, although they renounce them in their words. The result is a fundamental discrepancy between what idealists think and what they do: their philosophy is not a faithful reflection of their lives. Santayana is rightly adamant that we should not subscribe to views our acts belie; an honest philosophy requires unity of thought and action.

Realism, then, is the first great tenet of animal faith. Santayana's commitment to it is so firm that he thinks not even the objects of mind, essences, are mental or mind-dependent in nature, though this latter view is supported by observation and philosophical analysis, not the potent force of animal faith. But the possibility of action requires more than the realistic assumption of an independent world. Those alien objects and I must be continuous with one another, and each must be capable of affecting and being affected by all the rest. The threatening stranger and I meet downtown at a certain hour; if he had no access to me in space or time, or if he lacked the power to cause some ill effects, I would have little reason for concern.

A Single Field of Action

The independent objects of the world are deployed in space and time: they and my body constitute an unbroken field of action. The operations of the animal reveal that this field is the source of its woe and weal. There it must seek its food, avoid becoming prey, and fight now so it can live to fight another day. The notion of this spatiotemporal, energized field of action plays a central role in Santayana's thought. Belief in its existence, affirmed in every one of our acts, is the central commitment of animal faith. The philosophical implications of the idea are far-reaching. For if all existent reality is continuous with my body, everything capable of affecting me must lie in a single spatiotemporal matrix. If God and minds are effective agencies, therefore, they too must share the limits of life in space and time.

This is one of the crucial arguments which convinced Santayana that minds are impotent and that God cannot be both the ideal of perfection and a participant in the drama of the world. The latter point, along with his belief that religion is essentially symbolic in nature, inclined him to deny the existence of a God conceived along the lines of traditional Christianity. Santayana's self-proclaimed materialism also has its origin in his idea of the single field of action. For when he says that everything existent is material, he has no determinate and unalterable notion of materiality in mind. He is content, he assures us, to leave it to the physicists to tell us what matter is. His materialism, therefore, is simply the affirmation of the unity of the field of action and of the consequence that everything in it must be continuous with our physical organs. This continuity need not mean resemblance; such transformability as that of potential into kinetic energy or of energy into matter is adequate to assure it. The important point is that the spiritual, if in any sense effective, becomes a region in our field of action, explorable by the methods of science and eventually transformable into something we can grasp or see.

Santayana calls the unitary field of action "substance."[2] This word evokes scholastic or medieval connotations and has, accordingly, fallen into disrepute. Yet Santayana's use of it is appropriate and preserves the spirit of the Aristotelian tradition from which it hails. For substances were supposed to be enduring existents, bearers of potentialities, and centers of power. They were conceived as independent agencies never exhausted in what they do, the unified beings that display the features and traits we can discern. Aristotle himself thought that such substances were individual beings like Socrates or Xantippe's pet lizard. Santayana sometimes also writes this way, but in his more deliberate moments he makes clear that no single object in the physical world can have the independence required of a substance. Accordingly, he maintains that there is only one substance, the field of action itself, of which individual things are parts or, in the language of the tradition, "modes."

Belief in Objective Realities

The man I meet downtown has a definite nature. I may not know his habits and his thoughts; his menacing face may break into a smile when he sees the worry in my eyes. But his potentialities are firmly established and his power falls within settled parameters. His body maintains a fixed structure, his brain identifiable limits, his behavior stable patterns. In my actions directed toward him I assume that he is a precisely bounded force to reckon with, someone whose responses, though difficult to predict, arise from a distinct constitution. None of this, of course, means that he is easy to get to know, that he does not change, that the same structure never yields variable results. He is not forced to do what seems to flow from his nature, but his nature is there as the permanent source of what he does.

The structure or definite constitution of things is what the philosophical tradition has called their form. For Santayana, the skeptical reduction has already identified forms in their immediacy as the essences that are the objects of the mind. In the elaboration of his metaphysics, he shows that the forms of existing things are also essences. The reality of essences in their pure, unembodied condition can, of course, not be a tenet of animal faith: only existing things and their features are proper objects of the confidence displayed in what we do. But animal faith reveals to us a world structured by essences, objects with definite constitutions. This means that in acting we must reckon with certain facts, which we neither created nor can undo. The existence of such mind-independent and fully articulated facts is one of the assumptions of ordinary action.

The establishment of objective realities has great significance for Santayana's philosophy. It completes the subject-object distinction and renders it, in certain respects at least, absolute. Philosophers have from time to time supposed that the difference between the knowing subject and the known object was temporary or partial or drawn only for certain purposes. This view reached its greatest popularity among German idealists in the nineteenth century, but it is experiencing a resurgence today. According to it, the nature of objects, even if not their existence, is determined partly, largely, or altogether by the consciousness that comes in cognitive contact with them or by the linguistic or conceptual structures we employ. There is therefore no determinate world-structure, and hence no truth indifferent to the needs, interests, perspectives, language, cognitive apparatus, or operative purposes of the inquirer.

Belief in Facts and Truths

Santayana takes sharp exception to this view. The world is there, he thinks, to be discovered; it is not created or determined in the act of inquiry. To be sure, what we do can change things to a considerable extent. But when such action is intelligent and deliberate, it presupposes an accurate grasp of the facts prior to our intervention. With a superb sense for our experience, Santayana reminds us that nothing brings home the reality of objective facts, and thus of truth, with greater force than others lying.[3] Whether we can convince anyone of what really happened, whether we can demonstrate our innocence or our good intentions is then profoundly irrelevant to the truth we know and of which, in the eyes of religious people, God is witness. To this we can now add the growing number of bitter experiences with official, state-created "truths," which honest individuals know fly in the face of facts. Objective fact serves as the standard for our thoughts and words to approximate, and also as the starting point of actions aimed at accomplishing anything.

If we view these facts from the standpoint of the essences that structure them, they are objective truths. "Truth is simply fact," Santayana says, "though described under the form of eternity."[4] As constituents of truth, essences are not primary objects of animal faith. But what makes them parts of the truth is that they are embodied in the world. In this capacity they, or the facts they endow with form, hold central interest for agents in the flux: they are objects of animal confidence. It is only in disinterested inquiry, where the point is understanding not action, that the mind comes to know them as unchanging truths.

Ineradicable truth is the collection of essences materialized in the world or intuited by minds. Santayana thinks of it as the "silent witness" of the movement of existence, and "the wake of the ship of time, a furrow which matter must plow upon the face of essence."[5] In its totality, this complete record of all actual events is what he calls "the realm of truth," an infinite subset of the infinite realm of essence. As such, it is, at least in principle, always accessible to the mind, even though learning the truth about any particular thing and knowing that what we think *is* the truth present special problems. The idea of the realm of truth is a philosophical elaboration of the notion of objective fact. Although its reality is not a direct article of animal faith, the warrant for our commitment to it is that each time we act, we embody our belief in some parts of it.

I indicated earlier that the subject-object distinction in Santayana is in certain ways absolute. By this I do not mean, of course, that there is no contact or no relation between the two. It is just that the world is formed independently of any contribution by the mind. Since subject and object enjoy largely separate careers, there is no reason to postulate joint maturation or a final union and reconciliation. Admittedly, Santayana views the subject, in the form of consciousness, as the product of animal organisms. This could tie subject and object together by imprinting consciousness with the indelible mark of its origin. Santayana is keenly aware that the internal life tends to reflect the nature and predicaments of the physical creature that generates it. Yet he also notes that the immediate objects of consciousness, the essences which serve as the terms of that internal life, have no intrinsic or qualitative connection with their source. The result is that subject and object remain ever distinguishable and separate. They enjoy a twofold significant relation to one another: the material world generates the mind, and this mind sheds the cognitive light of consciousness on nature.

Individual Nature or Psyche

So far, we have concentrated on what beliefs our actions reveal about the external world. There are other convictions, about the agent organism and its cognitive apparatus, which remain to be explored. I want to begin with belief in two features of physical objects which relate them to the agent. The man I meet downtown is large and muscular. My actions aimed at avoiding him clearly indicate that I believe he has capacities and powers of significance to me. This, in turn, suggests belief in corresponding receptivities, even vulnerabilities, on my part. His size and disposition would be of little significance to me if he could not touch me or if hitting me were like punching a rock. In fact, however, I am easily affected and he has the power to take advantage of that.

There is also another side to this situation. As my bulking, potential nemesis approaches, I prepare for defensive action. I believe not only that he changes as he moves toward me, but also that he is changeable. He, too, is open to the influence of the external world; he may well alter his course as a result of what I do. This immediately indicates belief in the efficacy of actions and in my ability to perform them.

The point of human actions is to exploit the changeability of objects. To be able to do so, we must have limited but extensive operational capacities. My actions toward the threatening stranger indicate belief that I can kick and run and yell, but not fly. My behavior is appropriate to someone who holds that he may be hurt, that he can fight but probably not win, that he can strike the aggressor but in all likelihood not soon or hard enough. In this way, I impute a nature to myself, a set of vulnerabilities and powers no less definite than those belonging to the things I face.

Santayana uses the term "psyche" to refer to such individual human natures. Because of the everyday meaning of the related word "psychic," I must stress that there is nothing occult or spiritual about Santayana's psyches. He chose the word for its rich original significance in early Greek thought: there it was the name of the animating principle of the human body. The Greeks noted the striking difference between live and dead bodies and attributed it to the presence, in the former, of a power of self-generating motion. This power or "soul" was present wherever there was life: instead of operating out of some central location, it was suffused throughout the body. Although Plato supposed psyches to have a supernatural origin and destiny, the early Greeks saw no reason to introduce an ultimate, ontological distinction between them and the bodies they enlivened.

Body and Soul

In this last point, Santayana is in particularly vigorous agreement with the Greeks. Animal faith postulates the self as a combatant in the field of action. For each individual, it is the personal counterpart of the world of alien things he or she encounters, but from an objective standpoint, it is just another center of energy in a cosmos whose parts are unequally distributed.[6] As an agent in the field of action, the psyche is continuous with the rest of that field; this continuity assures that it is physical or material in nature.

Conceptualizing the issue in terms of the distinction between body and its animating principle, the soul, is good as a first approximation. But it has the disadvantage of inviting the misapprehension that body and soul are two separate entities. The emphasis on the materiality of the psyche is, of course, designed to deny this. Yet to eliminate even the possibility of supposing that human beings are somehow hybrids of two independent things, Santayana adopts Aristotle's conceptual framework and maintains that the soul is simply the body in its operational phase. This is tantamount to saying that the psyche is the form of the body, if form is taken not in its static sense as structure, but as a dynamic pattern of activity displaying itself through a stretch of time. Aristotle had something like this in mind when he talked about the soul as the first actuality of a natural body and remarked that if an ax were an organism, cutting would be its soul. This makes the psyche a collection of activities instead of a stagnant thing, and has immense significance for Santayana's treatment of the mind–body problem.

It is fair to say that, throughout his writings, Santayana speaks of the psyche in an ambivalent way: he likes to hypostatize and even to personify it, though in moments of philosophical care he reminds us that it is but a group of activities whose unity is mythological. Yet he never wavers in distinguishing the psyche from mind or consciousness, and since he is resolute in affirming its materiality, it is not inappropriate to assign it efficacy in the physical world. We need to note again that the subtleties of philosophical conceptualization are not what constitute the objects of animal faith: our action-carried belief is simply in our formed nature. The task of philosophy is first to uncover the tenets of animal faith and then to cast them in terms that enable us to give a consistent and satisfying account of the world and of our place in it. Failure in the second, very difficult task does not imply failure in the first.

Selectivity and Values

The nature my actions indicate I believe I have does not only or even primarily consist of receptivities and operational capacities. The stranger represents danger to me, and nothing could be threatening if I welcomed everything with equal delight. In fact, of course, I do not. There are some events I need or want to occur; others I go to great lengths to avoid. Dinner and a movie are on my downtown agenda, getting beaten or knifed is clearly not. Selectivity and preference constitute the heartbeat of the psyche: its every act expresses the established momentum of its animal life. The application of its powers itself is selective, designed to protect and promote its interests. The psyche is a directed charge of energy: it seems to know what to seek and what to shun, and how to find its way in a hostile or at best indifferent environment.

The preferences of the psyche provide, for Santayana, the foundation of all value. Although good, bad, and other moral qualities function as terms in consciousness alone, their organic counterparts in the psyche determine their occurrence and their objects. This simple and elegant idea enables Santayana to hold on to the irreducibility of moral terms while maintaining a sensible, naturalistic account of the generation of values. Santayana's theory of value (a phrase he disliked) thus closely parallels his philosophy of mind: here also he holds that empirically observable events serve as the ground of the right and the good, while such ideal outcomes perfect or complete their natural source.

In saying that the selectivity of the psyche is what underlies all valuation, Santayana explicitly refuses to accord any value the dignity or primacy due to noble origins. None comes to us through divine revelation, none is disclosed by rational intuition to be an objective feature of the natural world. Animal faith, moreover, does not in principle favor any value over others; its tenet is the general conviction that, in accordance with their individual natures, human organisms are selective in their preferences. This general belief is given determinate form in the situated actions of individuals. For my behavior expresses not simply the belief that I have sensitivities, powers, and values, but also that my jaw is easily dislocated, that I have a swift and nasty kick, and that I treasure both courage and bodily integrity. The specific content of such individual beliefs drops out when we try to determine the tenets of animal faith; all that remains is the determinable structure or generic meaning they share.

Knowledge

My actions indicate not only my belief in a sensitive, selective psyche endowed with certain capacities. They also reveal my conviction that it is intelligent. For intelligence is the effort to make response appropriate to situation or to apply one's powers to achieve desired results. That is the sort of responsiveness the psyche perpetually displays. And if intelligence involves the ability to read or use signs, so that we may get to know the absent by what is present to us, the psyche is a master at the art. From these considerations Santayana unhesitatingly concludes that the reality of knowledge is one of the beliefs affirmed by animal faith. Knowledge in this sense lays no claim to certainty. It is, according to Santayana's own definition, simply true belief mediated by symbols.[7]

Santayana pays no attention to an ambiguity in attributing knowledge to the psyche. The symbols that carry or "mediate" belief may be essences intuited or natural events. In his discussion of knowledge, Santayana limits himself to the first alternative: he holds, in this way, that cognition always involves the cooperation of psyche and consciousness. Yet some might think that he ought to consider the second alternative as well, because some sign-cognitive activity simply does not rise to the level of consciousness. I may, for example, leave the house and return at once for my umbrella without any explicit awareness of the movement of dark clouds in the sky. One might, in fact, suppose that it would be only knowledge of this sort, involving none but organic elements, that serves as a proper object of animal faith.

Yet Santayana is clearly right in not making some purely organic operation the paradigm of knowledge. Animal faith is unmindful of subtle ontological distinctions; for it, the difference between body and mind is not the sharp and ultimate affair it may become in a fully articulated philosophy. The trust of the animal, expressed in its actions, is that it can receive information, read the meaning of the sensory signs sent by the environment, and respond in an appropriate and advantageous way. The sensory signs constitute a goodly portion of what we call consciousness; there is no reason, therefore, to deny the role of awareness in the constitution of knowledge.

Animal response to ambient things reveals faith that the world is knowable and the belief that human efforts at unraveling its structure (or at least the structure of parts of it) can meet with success. The latter is at once the conviction that knowledge can be improved and that its object, the world at large, sets the standard by which its adequacy must be gauged. Whether we are bold experimentalists or unbending conservatives in what we do, we share the belief that intelligence can help us gain our ends. The major difference is only that innovation expresses the desire for better control, while established habit settles for time-tested results.

Knowledge is, in this way, primarily an instrument of life. Its ideal, Santayana points out, is to have the scope and precision of natural science which, whether it is used for that or not, permits greater foresight and more assured effects. Under no circumstances is knowledge the intuition of essence or the contemplation of timeless laws. The effort of inquiry, the mediation of symbols, the uncertainty of results suffuse it. When it is set free from the burdens and limits of its animal status, it loses relevance to time-bound truth and becomes an aesthetic construct, a free creature of the imagination.

Belief in Discourse

I have indicated before that the sensory signals involved in knowledge constitute the bulk of our conscious life. Belief in knowledge, therefore, implicates belief in a stream of awareness. Santayana's term for this process of internal life is "discourse." In ordinary language this word is used to refer to extended discussions or expositions. Santayana's meaning is similar, though restricted to consciousness. For him, in its broadest signification, discourse is the sustained movement of attention from essence to essence, what other thinkers have called the flow of ideas in the mind. In a narrower sense, discourse is the directed process of tracing implications or surveying evidence. The latter is a dialectical activity designed to enable us to reach conclusions about matters of interest to us. In both of its senses, discourse has essences for its terms and is thoroughly mental in its nature. The feelings and ideas it involves have no existence in a public space; only I have direct access to mine and only you to yours. This means that with belief in discourse, we complete on Santayana's behalf the movement from the objective world to subjectivity. There is, of course, more to be learned about the life of consciousness and some, at least, of this information can be grounded in animal faith. But before we proceed, it is important to note that even the subjectivity of the mind is, for Santayana, not purely subjective. Consciousness is always directed upon some object and those objects, the essences I spoke of before, are never mental. Although we enjoy privacy with our thoughts, the ideas we have, the themes we contemplate, the contents of our thoughts are always open to others to conceive.

Does animal faith posit knowledge and discourse in the agent self alone? Santayana is clear that it does not, but he thinks we cannot be as sure about the presence of mind in others as we can about our own consciousness. The reason is the misleading strategy of starting his constructive thought with solipsism of the present moment. The skeptic took his pursuit of certainty inside the self. The collapse of his quest left him with unmeaning data which, before the last gust of skepticism, had been objects of consciousness. Accordingly, in restoring belief on the basis of animal faith, Santayana first reestablishes the features and powers of the conscious individual. Only after this task is accomplished does he proceed to secure our knowledge of the existence and nature of the material world. He conceives of knowledge as essence-mediated cognition of physical objects; the thoughts and feelings of others, since they are on "the other side of the deployed events," become inaccessibly private episodes. They are not physical, so they cannot be perceived. They are not ours, so we cannot enjoy their immediacy. We thus have no compelling direct evidence to believe in any consciousness other than our own. Yet Santayana remarks that we have a "strong propensity" to suppose that others think and feel as we do.

The propensity is grounded in a naturally experienced version of what philosophers call the argument by analogy for the existence of other minds. I note that the substance, structure, and behavior of my body are closely paralleled by those of selected other portions of the world. Since my physical fortunes are accompanied by what appear to be appropriate feelings and perceptions, I readily conclude that similar events in others evoke a similar awareness.

Belief in Other Minds

This inference, though natural, is tenuous, and in *Scepticism and Animal Faith* Santayana finds it difficult to relate it to the faith we express in our actions. Yet in *The Realm of Matter* he unhesitatingly affirms that one of the presumable properties of the physical world is the presence in it of animals endowed with "feelings, images, and thoughts."[8] This suggests that he has a simpler access to knowledge of other minds than the argument by analogy.

If he started, as I have on his behalf, with the reality of animal action in the world, he would be entitled to equal confidence in the existence of consciousness in others and himself. For our actions reveal a differential attitude toward distinct parts of the environment. I am prepared to kick my downtown assailant but not the lava from the nearest volcano. This indicates not only intelligence in me, but the expectation of it in other animals. The kick I contemplate for the attacker is not meant to stop him the way a dam turns back surging spring waters. I know I have not the strength to accomplish that; but I can cause him pain and threaten more if he persists. In this way, I rely on his sensations, knowledge, judgment, anticipation, and concern; my action is structured to energize the faculties of his mind. My belief when I kick is not that he will be stopped but that, on the basis of intelligent assessment, he will stop himself. Santayana's caution that things mental are immaterial and therefore out of the reach of action should not concern us here. For, as we saw earlier, animal faith, the common sense of mankind, does not draw rigid ontological distinctions. And if the imperceptible future can be a proper object of animal confidence, which Santayana readily admits, there is no reason to suppose that the pains and thoughts of others cannot.

My argument brings Santayana more closely in line with his best intuitions and with the unreflective good sense of the human race. It does not imply that learning what others think is easy or that we can

ever know for sure when we succeed. To be confident that others have
feelings is not to know what those feelings are. Our inquiry into them
can never reach the status of science: it always remains in the realm of
the imagination as a part of what Santayana calls "literary psychology."

Belief in Memory

The response I make to the threatening stranger divulges my confidence in the veracity of memory. If I had never seen, heard of, or
found myself in similar situations and if I could not remember them,
I would have no guidance on how to act. A person arriving from some
pacifist planet could have no memories to help him detect danger and
would, therefore, take no steps for self-defense. My defensive posture
reveals my history and shows how much I trust my memories. Actions
based on such trust are, of course, no guarantee that all recollections
are true. The point is that memories are not radically flawed: I rely on
them in action and survive. I can feign doubt about them all, but I
cannot act on such universal suspicion. When I truly disbelieve a memory, my actions may show that, as well. But such a question about
some particular reminiscence must be embedded in a context of general
confidence; only by reference to trusted documents and valid recollections can a memory be challenged and declared mistaken.

Memories, when they are focused on our interaction with the world,
yield experience. In his characteristically felicitous way, Santayana defines experience as "a fund of wisdom gathered by living."[9] Our actions
expose our faith in the relevance of experience to life. Trust in experience is a complex affair: it involves belief in the psyche with a momentum of its own, in the environing world that supports yet often clashes
with the psyche, in the ability of the animal to survive this conflict
and to learn from it, and in the subsequent possibility of raising understanding and partial control over nature into an art. As such, faith
in experience recapitulates a number of our other beliefs. Its special
significance is that it relates them and exhibits their objects as parts of
an interactive whole. It is the process of experience that enables us to
attach meaning to what befalls us and to approximate the life of reason.

Belief in Intuition

Intuition is another object of animal faith Santayana discusses. He
comes to it early in his reconstruction of the edifice of human knowl-

edge and identifies it as the active principle in consciousness. Essences constitute the objects of our waking life, but since of an infinity of them only a few appear at any given time, they cannot be responsible for their presence. Intuition is the act which accounts for this show of essences; it is the light of awareness. It cannot itself be found in nature for it is not, in any sense, a physical process. Although the busy work of the psyche underlies it, intuition is a transparent, fleeting mental act.

It is difficult to see how intuition could be a direct object of animal faith. Our actions may well display our belief in the feelings, discourse, knowledge, and memory of people, but they cannot readily reveal our confidence that they have imperceptible acts that make their discourse possible. Admittedly, there must be such acts, but being implied by or required for objects of animal faith is to be distinguished from being such an object. I conclude that it is best to think of intuition as an indirect object of our animal trust. It is a part of the theoretical elaboration and completion of the philosophy of animal faith.

Philosophy and Common Sense

Santayana's exhilarating announcement in the Preface to *Skepticism and Animal Faith* is: "I stand in philosophy exactly where I stand in daily life; I should not be honest otherwise."[10] Just before the end of the book, he grows even more emphatic: "I should be ashamed to countenance opinions which, when not arguing, I did not believe."[11] His devotion to untangling the tenets of animal faith is the first and central element in his attempt to give "everyday beliefs a more accurate and circumspect form." He thinks that the "shrewd orthodoxy" of the human race is in its outlines correct, and it is to the defense of this timeless common sense that he dedicates his philosophical efforts.

Delightful as it is to hear a philosopher forswear abstruse and arbitrary dogmas, reflection may leave us with the feeling that whatever the skeptic had torn down has simply been restored. If this is true, honesty and common sense have been achieved at the cost of uncritical conventionality. But it is surely false. At the very least, Santayana placed what had been unexamined beliefs of dubious pedigree on the sound and unified foundation of animal faith. He also laid the groundwork for a philosophical edifice of remarkable scope, power, and coherence. And no one need be concerned about conventionality: San-

tayana's views of the mind, religion, and morality, all growing organ-
ically out of his philosophy of animal faith, contain searing surprises.
In what follows, we shall see that honesty in philosophy is compatible
with speculative sweep, conceptual rigor, and sound judgment about
the place of human beings in the world.

Chapter Four
The Changing World
Santayana's Mature Ontology

Santayana's mature thought, beginning with the publication in 1923 of *Scepticism and Animal Faith,* is cast in the form of a detailed and complete philosophical system. The backbone of the system is the four-realm ontology of essence, matter, spirit, and truth. The method supporting the ontology is discernment of the objects and analysis of the tenets of animal faith, along with careful observation of the facts of human experience. The former yield insights into the general structure of the world of action: into matter and certain associated features of truth and consciousness. The latter reveals the world of stillness, including the infinite reaches of the inactive realm of essence and connected characteristics of truth and spirituality.

The ontology was implicit in Santayana's earlier writing; even in his own opinion, it became only clearer and more deliberate in *Realms of Being.* This is not to deny that there are differences of detail and emphasis between the earlier work, written from the perspective of human experience, and the later books, which utilize cleaner, broader, and more objective categories. The frequently reported difficulty of getting entirely clear about the views developed in *The Life of Reason* may well be due to the fact that the ontology is only implicit there; Santayana's categories, properly understood, are powerful instruments of conceptual orientation.

The purpose of ontology is to identify and distinguish from one another the different sorts of being involved in our lives. One might suppose, of course, that there is only one kind of being; that, for example, in its basic structure and features everything real resembles atoms, galaxies, and apple pies. If so, one would be a rather narrow materialist and would have either to show that properties such as fatness and relations such as being-in-love-with are not real or to offer an account of how, against all odds, they can be features of an occasional collection of matter without characterizing its parts. But even if we

61

held such an improbable view, we would still have an ontology, albeit one unnecessarily impoverished.

The temptation to think that there is only one kind of being originates in commitment to a single paradigm or exemplar of reality. We may, for example, be so impressed with the causal powers of surging water and hurtling trucks that we quietly resolve to call nothing real that lacks some measure of the force and presence of these things. Such potent existents make quiet thoughts and mathematical relations appear pale and insignificant by comparison. As a result, we may readily suppose that they lack reality altogether and the only question is why we ever thought that they existed.

Reality Not Power

This is a perfectly understandable conclusion if we take reality to be identical with power: the mere fact that two and two make four has never caused changes in the physical world and my thought of a locomotive cannot pull a train. But there is no reason to embrace such a restrictive notion of reality. Whatever we encounter in our experience is obviously not nothing: if it fails to qualify as real by our preferred definition, then we have immediate evidence that there are other forms of being, as well. The lesson is to be attentive and let reality reveal itself. That different sorts of things are differently real does not imply that any of them is unreal or less real than the others.

We live in a world of things, and a great deal of our time is taken up with manipulating them. As a result, the category of the substantial, enduring object is preeminent in our minds. When we think of other forms of being, then, we naturally suppose that they must be quite like things, even though we know that they must be different from the things we deal with every day. This notion of a nonphysical object or thing wreaks havoc in ontology. It makes it impossible for us to develop a clear conception of genuinely divergent types of being. And it sets an illegitimate standard for ontological analysis, requiring that all its products share the crucial features of the sort of being most familiar to us.

Realms of Being

Santayana is keenly conscious of our tendency to hypostatize—to view as substantial and thing-like—all manner of ideas and reality. He

judges this tendency to be all the more dangerous because, in his opinion, physical objects do not constitute an irreducible ontological category at all. They are compounds analyzable into the ontologically
ultimate ingredients of essence and matter. Yet the language of ingredients itself leads us back to the conception of things: compounds made
of "ingredients" bring to mind such items as chocolate cake, which is
a physical object made of other ones. Santayana accordingly warns
against thinking of essence and matter as preexisting realities that
somehow unite to create the world we know. Such speculations would
constitute an ill-conceived cosmology or account of the origin of the
universe. Santayana's realms of being are not elements out of which the
world is made; they are distinguishable, irreducibly different features
of it as it exists fully constituted.

Accordingly, in spite of the possibly misleading connotation of the
word "realm," the realms of being are not portions of our cosmos or
worlds on their own. Essences, truths, spirits, and matter are not
beings in the manner of physical things, but elucidative categories that
help us think clearly about the most general features of the world.
"Spirit is a category, not an individual being,"[1] Santayana insists, and
although he sometimes writes as if the realm of matter were simply
identical with the physical world, a careful reading shows that he
thinks of matter as but one of the two irreducibly different elements
in existing things. "The Realms of Being," he says, "are only kinds or
categories of things which I find conspicuously different and worth
distinguishing," and he invites each person to "clean better, if he can,
the windows of his soul."[2]

This attitude of refusing to claim ultimacy for his ideas ties in directly with Santayana's individual relativism in cognition as well as in
morality. The character and adequacy of our values and knowledge are,
in his opinion, at least partly a matter of our circumstances and nature.
Agreement in either field presupposes a similarity of constitutions: the
oyster lives for other ends and views its watery world differently than
does the oysterman. Where nothing but difference connects two values
or two views, neither can claim superiority. Whatever windows open
from our souls, and whatever souls dwell in us, determine how we see
and what we seek.

I shall discuss these issues in greater detail in the next two chapters.
For now, let me stress that Santayana's relativism is by no means complete. The other side to the diversity of our natures is the identity of
the things with which we deal. There are objective truths about the

world—even if they are infinitely complex and difficult to get to know. Our ideas and our categories, if felicitous, are therefore not idle thoughts: there are features and structures in the real world that correspond to them. The notions of the realms of being are thus, like all ideas, essences envisaged or fancies in the private imagination. But they are also more: they are tools which, when wisely used, reveal the anatomy of the human world.

Primacy among the Realms

I have already indicated that the four realms of being are irreducibly different from one another. Yet they are not equally basic. Essence enjoys ultimate primacy, although not of course in any temporal sense. Time is constituted of a set of relations in the physical world and is therefore ontologically derivative; it has no relevance to the interrelation of the categories. Essence is primary because it serves as the condition of the possibility of the other realms: spirit and truth need forms in order to be, and even matter could not get past inarticulate potentiality without properties and relations to embody.

With respect to existence, primacy resides with the realm of matter. It is only matter that can make essences enter into external relations to constitute a contingent and changing reality. This immediately excludes the existential primacy frequently accorded to God and indicates that, for Santayana, the great question of why there is something rather than nothing cannot be answered by reference to rational principles or benevolent intentions. Without matter, no essences would gain embodiment: there could, therefore, be no truth. And conscious events are generated by complex changes in the physical world: the material psyche is indispensable to the existence of spirit.

If we view things from the standpoint of knowledge, spirit enjoys primacy. This does not mean that consciousness is the first or preeminent object of knowledge. On the contrary, Santayana clearly maintains that the primary and proper items of cognitive interest are the threatening and promising substances of the natural world. Spirit, in the sense of the intuitions directed upon essences, is known both last and least. In rare agreement with G. E. Moore, Santayana thinks that such conscious acts (as distinct from their objects) are diaphanous or transparent and thus their simple "intellectual essence" is difficult to capture. The primacy of spirit consists in its unique ability to know. The organic intelligence shown by living things is a pale replica of the cognitive power of awareness; without the light of consciousness, Santayana reminds us again and again, both the infinite realm of essence and the natural world would plunge into an insentient dark.

Since the four realms of being are not things or world-portions, the question of how they relate to one another to make a whole simply does not arise. They do not *constitute* the world, but serve as tools for understanding it. Conceptual orientation of the sort they provide is useful in reflecting on the fundamental characteristics of reality and in sensitizing us to the rich diversity of being. But the ultimate value of ontological analysis is the insight it yields into the human condition and the terms it supplies for an improved conception for the good life.

The Realm of Essence

Essences are timelessly self-identical forms or characteristics. By calling them "characteristics" I do not mean to imply that they are, or need to be, the features of anything. We do, of course, find essences serving as the properties and relations of physical objects, but that is not the only context in which we encounter them. We can also discover them in mathematical calculations, in aesthetic enjoyment, and in daydreams. Anything of which we can be directly aware, any immediately presented object of our thoughts is an essence. This might tempt us to suppose that essences have some intrinsic connection with intuition or mind, such as that all and only those things that can be conceived consistently are essences. But it is as groundless to maintain that every essence must be thinkable without contradiction as it is to insist that they must all be capable of being given material form. The idea of immateriality or the idea of God can obviously gain no embodiment, yet they are clearly essences. And Santayana unhesitatingly affirms that, although we cannot fashion a consistent conception of it, the square circle is nevertheless an identifiable form.[3]

In their intrinsic nature, therefore, essences are independent of both thought and existence. They are neither mental nor material; on the contrary, both the mental and the material are possible only by borrowing from the realm of essence and displaying their relevant and appropriate characteristics. Essences, in turn, are eternally available for such manifestation, though they do not lose their timeless self-identity either at the beginning or at the end of their embodiment. They are simply indifferent to what use mind and matter may make of them. This indifference is not like mine to the wart on your back; it is the unconcern of the equation $2 + 2 = 4$ to whether I wake up to think of it fondly in the night.

Santayana characterizes the realm of essence as " . . . a vast costumer's gallery of ideas where all sorts of patterns and models are on exhibition, without bodies to wear them, and where no human habits of motion distract the eye from the curious cut and precise embroideries of every article. This display, so complete in its spectacular reality, not a button nor a feather wanting or unobserved, is not the living crowd that it ought to be, but a mockery of it, like the palace of the Sleeping Beauty."[4] This image captures the richness of the vast, frozen reaches of the realm of essence. But it is not without certain misleading qualities. For no essence is, in its original nature, an idea. And while some forms are garbs for existence, many more are not and some can never be. The more we learn to think of essences in isolation from their role as providing qualities, relations, and structures for the world, the purer and more accurate our conception of the realm of essence will be. To accomplish this, it is best to let the imagination play with all manner of implausible ideas, with fanciful alternatives to our stolid status quo. Each of these notions is of course an essence, and in the democracy of the realm of essence none is inferior to the forms currently featured in the physical world.

Essences Eternal and Impotent

The eternity of essences may seem baffling, but it is not a very difficult idea. First and foremost, we must draw a distinction, inadequately appreciated in our churches and in ordinary discourse, between the eternal and the everlasting.[5] The everlasting is what exists in the time-bound world of our bodies and our hopes, and never ceases to do so. Atoms or the subatomic ultimate parts of matter are everlasting in this sense though, perhaps unfortunately, our kidneys and our hearts are not. The eternal, by contrast, never truly exists in time at all. It is exempt from the changes endemic to the world: while physical objects have a history of gradual and continued alteration, such eternal objects as the color yellow, when they appear in the spatiotemporal flux, do so like timeless apparitions without substance and without a past, ever untouched by the swirl of things. Time is simply irrelevant to the eternal, as is space: two and two add up to four with no reference to the person calculating. In the language of traditional Christian theology, God is eternal because His unalterable nature utterly transcends time. His Creation, or at least a part of it, is everlasting though exposed to change.

The fact that essences are eternal makes it impossible for them to exert physical power. Force requires the spatial and temporal contiguity of the cause with its effect; its exercise leaves not only the butt of action but also the agent changed. The notion of an eternal but efficacious God is, therefore, ontologically incoherent. If He is an effective force, Lucretius was right that He must be a part of the natural world. If He is eternal, He will always remain a physically impotent bystander, just another essence without causal or moral prerogatives. God as the being we ought to imitate is an eternal but physically powerless ideal. God as worldly force, if indeed there is such a power, is without the changeless perfection we adore.

What holds of God holds of all essences. But their impotence has an offsetting positive side: though they cannot cause changes, nothing can make them change. They are indestructible because, being in neither time nor space, they are inaccessible to the forces of the world. They shine like the distant stars, safe from the tumult and disorder of existence.

General and Specific Essences

Every possible thought evokes an essence and every phase of every physical being embodies one. Essences are forms of definiteness without which nothing could be anything in particular. Since definiteness is a matter of degree, essences come at all levels of specificity. The least determinate forms are at once the most general; increase in specificity entails the loss of scope. The essence color is relatively general, blue is more determinate, and azure blue of a certain shade is completely specific. Philosophers have traditionally looked with favor upon general forms; on occasion they have even denied that the fully specific has its own form at all. The reason for this was the understandable interest in getting clear about such important essences or definitions as those of humanity and justice. The generic forms were supposed to structure natural species or kinds of things; when correctly apprehended, they would reveal the inner nature of every member of the species.

There is something powerfully attractive about thinking of the world as populated by things that fall into neat and discoverable classes. The lines of demarcation between the living and the nonliving, beast and man, lord and peasant can then be supposed to be reassuringly uncomplicated. The human will always be human and justice will remain itself in every clime. General essences, if we think of them as holding sway over existence, confer upon it (as they did in Aristotle's system) some of the changelessness and assurance proper only to the eternal.

If a general essence lends nature to the species, it is easy to suppose that it sets the standard for it, as well. Humans are incorrigible in viewing everything in animate, purposive, and moral terms. As a result, the nature of a being can come to be seen as something not simply had but to be pursued, something that imposes tasks and in terms of which one's performance must be judged. This platonic development endows selected essences with normative force and lodges the answer to the question of what we ought to do in the species to which we belong and perhaps even in the class proper to us.

In the light of this complex and important intellectual edifice, we can readily see the disintegrative force of Santayana's ideas. If all essences are forms of definiteness, there is no reason to grant primacy or exclusive reality to general ones. The essence color is no more real and intrinsically no more important than the essence blue or even the multifold essences of its specific shades. And there is a form not only of humanity, but also of every conceivable individual. Actually, since individuals change in the course of their lives, there is an entire collection of essences, each slightly different from the next, for every one of us. The set that relates to me defines my total history; each member of it characterizes me at some time in my life, only to be replaced by another essence before long.

Essences Infinite in Number

The riches of the realm of essence, however, are greater even than this. For every form I embody at any given time, there are many others closely similar which I shun. If my weight at age forty is 150 pounds, there is another essence identical to the one I embody in every particular except that it has me weighing one ounce less. Such unembodied essences are frequently contemplated by weight-conscious people, and the least study of what diet books promise will convince us that there is an indefinitely large number of them. Each of my other characteristics can be varied as well, while we hold all or most of my other features stable; the permutations and combinations produced as we change one or more properties to a lesser or greater extent beggar the imagination. Each form of me can develop by using this strategy is an essence on a par with the one I actually display.

The same unavoidable multiplicity of essences surrounds our favored notion of humanity. If having a four-chambered heart is a part of that essence, there is another form that combines all our other shared features with a five-chambered center of circulation. Another essence of humanity comes into view if we suppose, as David Hume foolishly did, that all of us have a natural sympathy for the plight of others. Additional alternative essences can be brought before the mind by varying one or several of the properties that constitute what we think is *the* nature of humanity.

This line of thought reinforces Santayana's claim that there is an infinity of essences. But it also reminds us that, from the standpoint of their intrinsic nature, all essences are equivalent. None is more worthy of embodiment than any of the others and none, once instantiated, can earn continued existence by its excellence. This makes the embodiment of essences a function of contingency for matter and choice for human beings. Values are subsequent to existence and dependent on certain features of it; essences have no inherent value or perfection. They are not, in and of themselves, standards of anything, but they can become measures of achievement when adopted as the ideals of some existing being.

Implications of this View of Essence

Generic essences have no native superiority to specific ones and the simple among forms are no more primary than the complex. To suppose that there is but one essence for every existing species and that grasping it reveals the nature of a large number of individuals is to display both a failure of imagination and intellectual conceit. Imagination, if properly exercised, uncovers a jungle of alternative species-essences. And there is no solid ground for maintaining that any of these essences adequately captures the fundamental character of many existents. It is not, of course, that sorting creatures into kinds is impossible or without utility. But this is work of painstaking generalization based on exhaustive empirical study. In doing it, we must keep in mind the purpose of our labors, the rich variety of individual features we disregard, and the radical contingency of any essence, especially a general one, being embodied in the world. Most important, we must always remember that existence has no respect for rigid lines, that some individuals fit poorly in our classes, and that some may altogether escape categorization by whatever species-essence we care to use.

The discussion of the last few pages should make the power and implications of Santayana's conception of the realm of essence obvious. His articulation of the notion of essence may seem innocuous. But in fact it eliminates at one fell swoop the traditional notion of God, the unchanging universality and objectivity of values, the primacy of groups and species, the fixity of natural kinds, the necessity of existence, the inherent goodness or rationality of being, and the possibility of certain knowledge even about the most general things. His idea of the realm of essence foreshadows and determines all of the rest of Santayana's system. Essence, in this way, has absolute primacy not only among the types of being but also in Santayana's philosophy.

Essences of Events

There is one other application of the notion of essence we must consider. Essences are what philosophers call "universals": they are repeatable—and hence time-independent—characters, structures, or patterns. Species and individuals, properties and relations, things and persons all derive their nature from the essences they display. Santayana notes that events themselves are but patterns of the successive manifestation of properties and relations; as such, they too must have or be essences. His name for the essence of an event is "trope"; tropes, like all other universals, are eternal, repeatable patterns.[6]

The idea of tropes is immensely important for the development of Santayana's system, yet it appears to harbor a contradiction. If there is anything unique and unrepeatable, it is an event: it is unthinkable that the battle of Waterloo could actually take place again. And even if it somehow did, down to the last detail in a duplicate universe of horror and pain, *that* occurrence would not be the one now in our past, whose date schoolchildren are made to memorize. How, then, can the essence of the unique be repeatable? Is it not absurd to say that what is through-and-through temporal has an eternal form?

What appears as a contradiction is, when properly understood, the consistent heart of Santayana's position. Of course, there is a repeatable pattern events instantiate: every performance of *Hamlet* faithfully follows the text. Even greater uniformity of actual events can be observed in the successive screenings of a film and the nearly invariant waves that make for light. The objection that there might be minute unnoticed differences even among these occurrences is not to the point: the important consideration remains that there is no reason why the same pattern could not be embodied an indefinite number of times. Forms are, after all, not used up when they are used: any instantiation of any of them leaves it unchanged and whole, and thus open for adoption by the rest of the world. If every theater resolved to do nothing but *Hamlet* for a year, the play (as pattern) would still remain available for staging in my yard.

Tropes account for the orderly structure of events, for the precise nature and succession of their parts. Since they are repeatable universals, however, they cannot explain how occurrences can be unique. Yet actual happenings clearly are: each of two identical performances of *Hamlet* is precisely itself and somehow different from the other. We might be tempted to suppose that this singularity derives from the time and location of the performances. But spatial and temporal relations are themselves repeatable essences and therefore cannot confer unique individuality on anything. The unimaginably complex trope that is the history of this world contains within it all our spatial and temporal relations; this essence is itself repeatable and could be embodied, as Nietzsche believed it actually has been and will be, again and again.

The Realm of Matter

No essence, nothing that is a form, can bestow uniqueness on events. Individuation is the work of another factor; it is due to the sheer fact that certain events *occur*. When of a large number of possible happenings one actually takes place, the difference between the trope embodied and the essences left out is nothing formal: it is simply what Santayana calls "the insane emphasis" of existence. There is no structural or qualitative distinction even between a trope and that same trope embodied; the difference, like that between the possible and the actual, is the absolute one of existential status.

The difficulty with this difference is that words, even thoughts, cannot capture it. Articulating it would involve the identification of features in the one that are absent in the other, and all such features are essences. Existence, by contrast, is not a character or quality; it is sheer material presence. The presence can be pointed to, encountered and physically engaged, but there is nothing we can say about its brute existential element. This is what Santayana means when he says that existence is a surd: it is the unintelligible, unutterable force that wrenches essences out of their placid eternity to give them actuality for a day.[7] Language and mind apprehend the forms of things; our bodies are left to deal with their matter.

The brute force that renders essences existent is what Santayana calls "matter." In a sense, of course, even the minimal designation of it as a force is misleading: any such notion evokes only essences and no form is adequate or even relevant to what can be referred to only as the formless other of essence. The fitting and beautiful capstone to this line of argument is Santayana's conclusion that existence escapes or transcends even its own essence. For the essence of existence is just another essence: it cannot bring about its own embodiment and it cannot exhibit what in matter is responsible for the surge of actuality. Accordingly, Santayana declares existence in general, and with it the coming into being of every existent, unintelligible. In speaking of matter, he reverts to the traditional strategy of those who reach the outer limits of the human mind: he substitutes symbols and analogies for a direct cognitive attack. He invites us to think of matter as the whirlwind that sweeps essences into the vortex of existence, as primal will, and as the breath of selectivity.

Existence a Surd

When Santayana says that existence is incomprehensible, he does not mean that we learn nothing about the world by careful attention to the causal order. We can trace the customary sequence of events and doing so endows us with a measure of foresight and control. We can form useful and accurate generalizations about conjunctions. We can frame bold theories about the broadest correlations. But in any sequence we know only the terminal points of change; the generative bond between them remains obscure. Why should one event make room for another? Why should scratching my nose be followed by pleasure instead of the decomposition of the organ? We simply accept things the way they come; we may even grow indignant at people who question the overt order of nature and suggest that there may be more to know. But our imagination, stimulated to take a fresh and distant look, disintegrates complacency with the familiar and shows us the radical strangeness of whatever occurs. We can answer the practical question of what follows what, but never the deeper one of why.

Since he thinks all knowledge is symbolic, it may seem unremarkable that Santayana resorts to images and analogies to communicate his idea of matter. Yet there is an important difference between symbolic cognition of the world and the picturesque representation of matter. The physical world is, for Santayana, fully formed: it embodies an essence or a set of essences in each of its parts. In using symbols to gain knowledge of it, we employ intuited essences to disclose embodied ones. In attempting to give an account of the nature of matter, however, we utilize essences to obtain a measure of insight into the unformed. From the purely cognitive standpoint, this enterprise is doomed from the start. Nevertheless, it is of value in putting the oft-experienced mystery of existence in a broader, philosophical context and in giving us some idea of why ultimate knowledge of reality is impossible.

Matter and Substance

There are places in Santayana's voluminous writings where he does not draw a clear distinction between the realm of matter and the world of substance. Starting from these passages, commentators have wrongly supposed that, for Santayana, "substance" and "matter" are synonymous. A careful reading of the texts and a full articulation of Santayana's ontology makes it clear that these two concepts are different in important respects.[8] "Substance" in its proper signification refers to the formed physical world or to significant parts of it; as in Santayana's master, Aristotle, this substance is a compound of form and matter. Independent thinghood, which is the idea central to substance, plays an indispensable role in cognition and action. The notion of substance, therefore, is primarily epistemological–practical in importance and derivation.

The idea of matter, by contrast, is frankly ontological. Its function is to help us understand the different modes of being, not to call attention to the nature of the world in whose bosom we live. The ontological idea of matter is a necessary ingredient in the fully developed notion of substance; all substance, Santayana points out, is material. The fact that he speaks of the "realm" of matter may well contribute to the misapprehension by evoking connotations of a world or region. But I have already addressed the inappropriateness of taking ontological realms to be anything of that sort; all I can do here is to warn again that ontological analysis slices the world into types of being, not into existing chunks.

What does Santayana's materialism come to in light of this view of the realm of matter? It remains the now fully developed position of the generative primacy of matter. The implications of the doctrine are far-reaching and easily identified as traditional companions of materialism. If matter is the source of all existence, no creative role is left for God. If matter is unformed and hence unconscious, the world is contingent to the core and at best indifferent to our values. If matter lacks rational structure, knowledge is a piecemeal achievement and can never be complete. In this way, the rejection of theism and of an anthropocentric world, and the embrace of chance, of empiricist fallibilism and of the final meaninglessness of human life are natural consequences of materialism. Santayana's pessimism about our ultimate prospects is grounded not in his aesthetic vision of the spiritual life, but in his unflinching judgment about the realities of the material world.

The Realm of Truth

Once we have a clear conception of essence and matter, understanding the realm of truth should present no difficulty. For truth is simply that portion of the realm of essence which matter, in the history of the world, selects for actualization. There is no particular unity to this realm, just as there is none to that of essence: the miscellaneous forms that have been, are being, and will ever be given momentary actuality all belong to it. Like essence, truth is eternal even though it is always the truth about what takes place in time. Matter forges ahead and creates new facts, yet the truth about what is to be has forever been part of a changeless realm. This does not mean that the future is unavoidable or foreordained, only that on the level of essence there is no becoming. Whatever essence will have graced existence has always been included in the truth, even though its embodiment may now seem distant and tenuous.

This can be seen more easily if we think of the entire realm of truth as a single, infinitely complex essence. By varying one or several of its elements, we get an infinite string of alternative truth-essences. From the standpoint of our position in time, we can already know that some of these essences are not the realm of truth, for something that happened in the world does not accord with their ingredients. Others among the alternatives can still turn out to be the intricate form of truth, though there is no sure way of predicting which *one* matter will have picked out in the end. The future is open: existence is under no compulsion to select any essence over all the others. And our ignorance is understandable; since the future is as yet undetermined, it is impossible to know it. Yet of all the alternative truth-essences, each minutely different from its neighbors, one *is* the realm of truth and, since it is an essence, it is that unchangingly.

Truth Objective

The discussion so far clearly implies that truth is independent of our knowledge of it. In fact, not only do perception, inquiry, and consciousness not create the truth they explore, it is the objective truth that makes our true opinions possible. For to know or speak the truth is to repeat one or more of the essences that constitute it; without this independent standard, human beliefs would be a web of rumors and fabrications. And even if there were no minds and no knowledge, the reality of truth would be unaffected. For truth is indifferent to being known; it is the silent witness of what happens in the world, the unerasable record of all events. Santayana calls it "frozen history."[9]

The fact that he thinks our beliefs are true when they capture one or more of the essences that constitute the truth about their subject suggests that Santayana endorses what philosophers call "the correspondence theory of truth." According to this view, true ideas re-create in our minds the very forms, or something close to the forms, embodied in reality; all other ideas fail to do so. This correlation or correspondence of forms does not make consciousness fade into identity with its object. On the contrary, the form is instanced twice: once in the world and once in the very different mode of being that is proper to the mind. It is just that, under favorable circumstances, what are from the standpoint of existence two become formally, essentially, or qualitatively identical: the idea in the mind becomes an accurate replica of reality.

Symbolic Truth

Santayana does, indeed, hold that the ideally true belief replicates the essence embodied in the world. But he hastens to add that the discrepancy in scale between our senses and the ultimate units of physical reality makes it extremely unlikely that such qualitative identity is ever achieved. Moreover, even if it were, we could never know it, because there is no way of comparing the essence in consciousness with the physical form it is supposed to duplicate. These considerations suggest to Santayana the essential irrelevance of the ideal of correspondence. An appropriate symbol is adequate, he maintains, for the purpose of cognition. Moreover, it has the advantage, so long as we remember that it is a symbol, of not tempting us to suppose that we are in direct contact with, and perhaps even in direct possession of, reality.

In what sense is symbolic knowledge of existence true? Santayana calls the truth about any fact the standard comprehensive description of it. Although "description" misleadingly suggests human activity, which as we saw has no essential connection with truth, Santayana is clear that he refers by that word only to the essences that articulate the fact, not to our grasp or use of them. The truth is "standard" in two senses: it is the objectively accurate, unbiased "description" of the fact and it serves as the ideal human opinions aim to approximate. It is by reference to the comprehensiveness of truth that the validity of sign-cognitive activity must be understood. For Santayana thinks that the truth about any fact includes vastly more than the essence or set of essences which define its narrow perimeters. He speaks of it as consisting not only of essences locally embodied but also of all the relations in which that fact stands to other facts, essences, and minds. Although the relations of facts are richest perhaps with their spatial, temporal, and logical neighbors, and tend to "grow thinner" with increasing distance and irrelevance, this still makes for an infinite number of truths about every one of them.

Truth Infinitely Extended

The truth about Washington hugging his wife after his inauguration, for example, includes more than the complex essence of the two intertwined. It is also true that this happened after they were married and before they died, in North America and not in the Congo, in front of people but not of water buffaloes. More trivially, it is true that Washington was not an Indian, a Martian, a type of yeast, a rare comet, or the number seven; he hugged his wife and did not choke her, scalp her, or make her fly at the speed of light; and he embraced *her,* not a water snake, fried liver and onions, or the Andromeda galaxy. To be sure, such truths may seem too frivolous to be worthy of the name. But this reveals only our veneration of truth: we think of it as a rare, precious, and important possession. Yet nothing is more common than truth, and those who wish to be sure that most of their statements are true ought to recite the multiplication table a few times every day. What is trifling and what carries vital significance are determined by our needs and interests: momentousness is not an intrinsic feature of the truth.

Facts are related to minds by evoking in them the intuition of certain essences. The way in which any fact appears to a consciousness is only partly a matter of the nature of the fact; the rest is governed by the structure and circumstances of the mind. In symbolic cognition, it is true that the essence present in awareness is not identical with that exemplified in the fact. But it is undeniably true also that to a mind of a certain constitution, operating under definable conditions, this is the way that fact appears. Appropriate symbolism is true, then, as just that: the cognitive reaction of a consciousness utilizing whatever terms are available to it.

The scope, accuracy, and adequacy of such true beliefs are, of course, issues separate from their status as truths. Since the truth about any fact is vastly complex, symbolic knowledge (along with any other type there might be) succeeds in capturing only a small portion of it at a time. If by "accuracy" we mean exact replication of the essence embodied, symbolism neither needs to nor is likely to accomplish that. And the adequacy of sign cognition is a function largely of our aims: rich, picturesque descriptions work better in poetry, austere mathematical symbols yield more fruit in science. The ultimate test here consists in the actions we can perform and the results we attain. A remarkable passage at the end of *The Realm of Spirit* gives an apt illustration of Santayana's generous, if not permissive, attitude to the truth of our beliefs. In discussing wrongheaded objections to his thought, he asks if his critics' representation of his work is fair. Astoundingly, he answers, "I think it is, in the sense that such a photograph might be taken of my system in a bad light at a great distance."[10]

The Realm of Spirit

The realms of essence and truth enjoy undisturbed, eternal being. The realm of matter, by contrast, is the source of temporal, changing, unstable existence. There is an intermediate mode of being with which we are all familiar and which Santayana calls "spirit." It takes the eternal as its object and has the temporal as its source; the acts in which it lives are internally changeless, yet their form of being, actuality, is tenuous and evanescent. Matter is the home of power, essence of passive indifference; spirit is impotent but yearns for efficacy and suffers the pain of its vulnerable state.

Santayana is keenly aware that the word "spirit" evokes connotations of incorporeal or even ghostly persons. This accords with his intentions at least in part: he thinks that mind is immaterial. But personhood suggests substantive being, and Santayana vigorously rejects the notion that the mind is a sort of disembodied thing. We cannot know for sure why he chose this word to designate the realm of mind, though we can make some reasonable conjectures. In the early drafts of the *Realms of Being* series, he had favored the term "consciousness."[11] But he abandoned this word, perhaps as too bland or Hegelian, by the time the books actually appeared. "Mind" always struck him as overly intellectual and in disrepute as a result of the use made of it by Absolute Idealists. "Soul" reminded him of Aristotle's "psyche" which, at least as an agency in the material world, he thought had already been accommodated in his system. With all its liabilities, "spirit" offered one decisive advantage over all the other words: it pointed in the direction of the proper function or perfection of the mind. Spirit in its purity is spiritual, that is, absorbed in the contemplation of essence. This is a critically important point for Santayana's philosophy, and it is a natural one to make if we use the word "spirit" for something very similar to what we normally call consciousness.

When we first find spirit, it is not in its spiritual phase. Its station and daily rounds involve it in the business of life, for it is the conscious expression of the battles and fortunes of the psyche. Since it is but the psyche come to knowledge of itself, it embraces the concerns of the body. Because initially it fails to note its separate identity, it may even suppose that it is an agent in the field of action. Although spiritual immersion in the immediate is possible at any stage of life, full self-understanding on the part of consciousness is attained with difficulty through spiritual discipline and constant reflection.

Intuition

The basic unit of spirit is the intuition, which is an act of consciousness directed upon essences. Intuitions are essentially cognitive: the presence to them of objects is not spatial, and their grasp of them is intellectual, not physical. Such presence or presentation is the essence of consciousness and thus, as a categorically ultimate fact, not much can be said to describe it. Of course, we experience it every day and can readily focus it in the mind by thinking of such dissimilarities as that between physically eating a steak and imagining that we do. Santayana's own suggestion is that we conceive of awareness as "the total *inner* difference between being awake or asleep, alive or dead"; this disparity should help us identify the indefinable but familiar cognitive nature of our minds.[12]

Intuitions consist of simple, unitary acts. The object of each is an essence or set of essences of some complexity. The act takes in its essences at a single glance and thereby confers a measure of unity on them. This is what Santayana means when he speaks of the synthetic nature of consciousness: at each moment of its operation, a multiplicity of elements appears to the mind as a single, unified whole. The combinatory power of awareness makes the presentation of any genuine succession impossible; for this reason, time cannot be intuited. The synthesis eliminates passage, and before and after become coeval ingredients in a specious present. The real succession of past, present, and future is reduced to a perspective in which the elements neither lapse nor change. Since time cannot be an immediate object of awareness, Santayana concludes that nothing given or directly presented exists. The sequence of events of which the physical world consists is revealed to us through animal faith; if the belief-element is removed, immediate consciousness shows only tropes with painted or aesthetic vistas of time and space.

Belief or Intent

Animal faith appears on the level of spirit as intent. Organisms beset by cycles of hunger and need have a natural urge to believe. This physical impulse has a mental counterpart or expression: the powerful tendency to take the data of sense as signals of outlying objects. Intent is just this inclination to believe or to utilize the given to yield information about physical facts. Without intent, knowledge would be impossible, even though the flow of intuitions could go on unabated. When intent is present, however, intuition can never be pure, for then essences, instead of being enjoyed for their own sake, come to be used as means to learning about the world. The primary obstacle to attaining the spiritual life is, therefore, intent that is in the service of interest in utilitarian or practical affairs. This impediment to pure intuition is by no means accidental and readily removed. On the contrary, the pre-

carious life and time-bound condition of the animal make concern for
its welfare compulsory. And the spiritual life can never become a mode
of existence; pure intuition, like a distant song, rises but intermittently above the smoke and din.

We have already seen that Santayana thinks physical time is never a
direct object of awareness. The distance between time and consciousness is, however, even greater than this: he maintains that mental acts
themselves can be said to be in time only "by courtesy." Since claims
like this appear implausible, it is important to understand the reasoning that leads to adopting them.

Spirit Not in Time or Space

Intuition is a simple, cognitive act. Accordingly, its actualization
has an all-or-none quality. Each time the act occurs, it does so completely and at once; the alternative to instant completion is no actualization at all. This is in sharp contrast with the natural processes of
physical agency. Building a house or reading a book are not instantaneous achievements; they take time to accomplish. There is an internal
diversity to such processes: their beginning, their middle, and their
end are distinct deeds supplanting one another in orderly succession.
Time, which is but sequential replacement, gnaws at the heart of such
performances; although we are inclined to say that they occur or are in
time, it is more accurate to note that time in the form of passage is *in
them.* In one sense, such processes are never complete. When we begin
them, their end is in the future; when we reach consummation, everything that led us there is long dead and past. In the world of processes,
time infects our acts and serves as the medium of loss and death and
failure.

In the activity of consciousness, by contrast, there is no internal
diversity. The beginning, middle, and end of a stretch of quiet joy at
seeing the sun set are not distinguishable by intrinsic marks; it is only
when we measure this happiness against external physical processes,
such as the movement of the sun or of a clock, that phases can be
imputed to it at all. In fact, of course, the imputation is misleading
because my delight is identical and complete at each moment of its
occurrence. Such activities, in the Aristotelian sense on which Santayana relies, represent the only unfailing achievement open to us: there
is no uncertain development, no passage, and no loss as the joy en-

dures. Intuition is an act with no time in it. It is our only hope for transcending the flawed mortality of all we do.

The transcendence is, of course, not physical or personal or lasting. Measured by the external standard of the physical world, it is short-lived and insubstantial. In achieving it, we surmount personality, as well. But it is the one perfect thing we can do, and it raises us to a level of actuality which is the closest approximation of existence to eternity.

The fact that intuition is an act dependent on material developments implies that it occurs *at* a time. But even this date of it is assigned on the basis of comparison with external processes. Internally considered, intuition has no natural temporal location at all; by examining it alone, we could never determine where in the history of the world, if anywhere, it properly belongs. This temporal homelessness of intuition is paralleled by its spatial unlocatability. Since it is a simple, cognitive act that lacks physical coordinates, it cannot be found even in or near its generative organ. Although the philosopher Locke was right that when one goes from Oxford to London one does not leave one's mind behind, this does not mean that it can be met with near the driver in the car. We should not allow preoccupation with physical objects to blind us to the variety of being. When I travel, the truths about me are also not left under my pillow back home. Yet that does not mean that they accompany me in the manner of my dog and its pesky fleas. Minds and truths are not abandoned for the same reason they are not found with flashlight or microscope: they do not inhabit space. Those who search for consciousness had better be satisfied with finding its organ.

A Multiplicity of Intuitions

All acts of intuition have the same simple essence. How, then, can there be many intuitions and what distinguishes each from all the rest? The acts are multiplied by their organs, which are complex physical structures. From the standpoint of its origin, consciousness is a completely dependent product of the psyche. *Total* reliance is a difficult relation to conceptualize. The dependence of an infant on its parents is not complete, for children—no matter how young—have a measure of self-generating life. Even chemical reactions are not point-events, but display some self-sustaining momentum. Each individual mind, by contrast, is generated one intuition at a time. As activity or all-or-none event, the intuition bursts into being and then is gone without trace or residue. That is the way our thoughts disappear and, when they remain for awhile, it is only because the psyche resuscitates them from moment to moment relatively unchanged.

Internally, moments of consciousness are differentiated by the essences they envisage. Recognition of this is the ground of the romantic notion that the minds of distant lovers can unite by sharing a feeling or embracing the same idea. In such cases, the identity of the essence intuited is supposed to obliterate the distinction and overcome the separateness of these ardent souls. Something like this can actually take place, but the union is only thematic, never actual. The two acts can share an object and thus achieve an identity that is, internally and qualitatively, total. But so long as the lovers are physically distinct, so long as two psyches generate consciousness, there will always be two separate intuitions. Material reality sets limits even to our ideals.

These are the four realms of being Santayana distinguishes and whose conception he develops in his mature system. Even though he readily admits that three of the realms (essence, truth, and spirit) are immaterial and two (essence and truth) are nonexistent, he does not think that such an ontology is at odds with the common sense his philosophy of animal faith is meant to explicate. Admittedly, our daily lives are saturated with concern for success in dealing with the material forces of the world. But we also experience moments of quiet contemplation and of lyric joy, we dream and do pure mathematics, and we seek the truth though it may lead to our ruin. The philosophy of animal faith must acknowledge the generative primacy and the overwhelming power of the world of action. It must carry the analysis of that power beyond the knowledge or the skill necessary to fend it off. And it must do justice to those actions and those thoughts that represent the higher reaches of human imagination and achievement.

Analysis of Change

To show the power of these categories, let us look at the analysis they make possible of change and of our perception of it. In Santayana's opinion, change is endemic to the world and it is always physical in nature. To say that it is physical means that it involves substance, which is a composite of matter and essence. Alteration, then, is a relation between matter and at least two essences. Let us suppose that one of the two characterizes a region of matter at a given time; change occurs if the second essence replaces the first in that region at some immediately succeeding time. Change, therefore, is simply the exchange by existence of the forms it adopts.

Santayana is aware that we could not properly speak of change without persistence or continuity. If one essence displaced another, totally different and unconnected one, each would articulate a world with no detectable passage from the first to the second. Alteration can take place only in a context of relative permanence: if many or most things remain the same, some few qualities and relations may be modified. Santayana can offer two ways of conceptualizing this continuity through change. We may view permanence as the prolonged embodiment of the same essences and mutation as the exchange in that context of a select few. Or we may think in terms not of isolated essences but of hugely complex ones, each slightly different from the next. On this analysis, only one form is embodied at any one time in the total situation; it is succeeded by another, different from it in minor particulars. The permanence is measured by the overwhelming similarity of the two complex essences, the change by their small divergences. Analytically inclined scrutiny, such as we find in science, might favor the former account; poetic souls, looking for broad vistas and organic connections, would find the latter congenial. In either case, however, though changes may display regularity, there is no necessity that they take place. Matter tends to fall into habits and repeat its performances. Yet since it is moved neither by cosmic purpose nor by unalterable laws (which are but impotent essences), all it does is gratuitous and contingent.

Analysis of Perception

In the attempt to account for the nature of perception, philosophers frequently fall into opposite excesses. Some think that when we perceive, we experience or are in direct contact with the surface of material things. Others maintain that physical objects are made of the sensory qualities of perceptual experience. The former view constitutes the mind, or at least a part of it, out of material elements; the latter constructs the physical world out of the stuff of private sensations. In the process of relating mind to matter, neither view preserves the separate integrity of each.

Santayana is particularly careful not to let relation destroy identity.

The experienced diversity of self and world can be maintained, he thinks, only if the contact between them is not immediate. Accordingly, his analysis of the perceptual relation involves three, instead of the usual two, major terms. In all perception there is a cognitive act, an immediate object of consciousness, and an unpresented object of intent. The act is an intuition, its direct object is an essence, and the item we know by means of it is a portion of material substance.

The psyche is constantly subject to the influence of the environment. Some of the impact of the external world rises to consciousness in the form of intuitions. Intent or animal faith naturally takes the essences presented in intuition for signs of material agencies. The utilization of essences evoked under the press of physical give-and-take for the purpose of learning about ambient forces constitutes perception. Such sense-experience is true if there is indeed a physical object in the region we explore and if the intuited essence is an apt symbol for it. If there is no relevant physical object present, as in the case of hallucinations, or if the essence cannot be employed as a useful symbol, as in the case of sensory qualities presented under the influence of drink, the attempt at perceiving does not succeed.

Perception is a form of knowledge. Its object, therefore, is always some existing thing, not an intuited essence. The essence "mediates" the knowledge: it is the means which, when used as a symbol, enables us to gain some grasp of the location, nature, and tendencies of physical forces. It is only by the rarest of accidents that the intuited essence and the form embodied on the surface of the physical object coincide exactly. Even if that happens, the identity is only qualitative, not numerical: although we may deal with the same form, it is instanced twice. But such qualitative identity is not necessary for the purpose of knowledge or of action; whether I see the moon as a luminous crescent or an opaque spheroidal satellite makes little difference, so long as the content of each of these perceptions ties in with a broader system of cognitions and helps make our actions intelligent and appropriate.[13]

Philosophers who think that in sense experience we achieve direct contact with the surface of physical objects have great difficulty in explaining error in perception. For their view obliges them to hold that either nothing sensuous is present to the mind, or whatever lies before us is a physical surface as it exists in nature. In the former case we cannot suppose that we are perceiving, in the latter it is impossible for us to be wrong. It was the recognition of difficulties such as this that motivated a number of American philosophers to publish a collaborative volume, *Essays in Critical Realism,* in 1920. The view, variants of which they espoused, is realistic in the sense that it affirms the existence of a mind-independent world, and critical in that it rejects the naive assumption that our contact with it is immediate. Santayana contributed an essay entitled "Three Proofs of Realism" to this book. His analysis of the perceptual situation makes an account of sensory error elegantly simple: it occurs whenever the relation of the object of intuition to the object of intent is inappropriate. This explanation takes seriously the experiential fact that whenever we think we are perceiving, there is some sensory content before the mind. It is just that this essence does not stand in proper symbolic connection with material reality.

There are three realms—essence, matter, and truth—involved in Santayana's analysis of change. Since perception is a conscious activity, his discussion of it is framed in terms of all four realms of being. Even my brief sketches of his approach should show the clarity and force of the accounts his categories make possible. His conceptual framework enables him not only to shed light on these difficult and apparently isolated problems, but also to overcome their disconnectedness by placing them in the broader context of interrelated general ideas. And, significantly, the ontological richness of his realms aids him in avoiding the simplistic and reductionist mistakes of some other thinkers. Let us now see how the application of the categories assists him in dealing with problems of more pressing human concern, whose solution philosophy has a special duty to attempt.

Chapter Five
Human Natures
The Natural and the Ideal

The theme pervading all of Santayana's work on the moral, aesthetic, and spiritual dimensions of the good life is the organic connection between nature and fulfillment. The good, the beautiful, and the divine are not eternal, autonomous forces that compel our attention or obedience. They are the ideals existence sets before itself when it reaches a certain complexity and flowers into mind. Our nature determines what will fulfill it and it is only by the efforts of the natural creature in us that that consummation can be attained. Values, therefore, are not alien standards to whose authority we submit grudgingly; they represent a conscious expression of what we can and naturally strive to be.

If our nature defines the perfection possible to us, the deliberate pursuit of excellence requires knowledge of our nature. Santayana agrees with the Greeks that an accurate assessment of who we are is of primary importance if the good life is to be consciously pursued. Such self-knowledge is difficult to achieve not only because of the complexity of its subject, but also because of the dishonesty of the self with itself. We tend to deceive ourselves about our motives and powers and prospects, and to convert our hopes into fervently accepted creeds. We think ourselves "too good for extinction," so we invent a supernatural origin and an immortal destiny for our souls. Since we cannot accept our modest station in nature, we fabricate a picture of the world that places the human race or the petty human self at cosmic center-stage. Individual candor and proper self-understanding cannot be achieved without a sound general portrayal of the place of human beings in the world. The heart of this account is the view we take of the relation of the mind to the body.

Body and Mind

The distinction between body and mind has been with us since the dawn of Western civilization. It is not a disjunction created by religious passion; on the contrary, its experiential foundation has always served as a source and support of religious sentiment. It is, of course, true that the so-called mind-body problem is a creature of the conceptual framework or the theories we adopt. But a careful look at our daily experience and the fact that the problem haunts the history of Western philosophy indicate how very natural and how appropriate it is for us to think in this way. The burden of proof is not on those who maintain there is a distinction between mind and body, but on thinkers who assert that the difference is illusory.

Our ordinary experience reveals a world in which everything has a place and everything can be found. It is a world in which simple presence and reality coincide: whatever has location in it is a substantial, independently existing thing. Such things enjoy a measure of efficacy, which they exercise without a sense of self and without feeling. They are compounded of parts each of which, like the cut halves of a worm, is capable of an autonomous career. The alert observer can trace the movements of these parts and occasionally modify them to obtain desirable rearrangements.

Some elements in our experience do not fit in the spatial, physical world. The feelings of others cannot be found and our own are mercifully private. Hopes and desires enjoy an intermittent existence that waxes and wanes with the movement of attention. Our ideas of wealth are impotent to swell our bank accounts. To thought, presence and substantial reality are often separate affairs: the long dead, the evanescent, what will never exist inhabit our minds. Anger and love are not compounded out of parts; they are simple unities in experience that may come unbidden and then disappear without a trace. No one has direct access to beliefs to destroy or to modify them. And nothing even remotely analogous to our inexpressible subjectivity or sense of self can be found, or even reasonably conceived, to exist in the material world.

The natural conclusion is that there are two significantly different sorts of being: conscious, private, nonspatial minds, and public, extended, and insensate physical objects. Early in the history of thought, this sensible and defensible distinction became associated with the dubious thesis of the preeminent power of mind. The reason for assigning efficacy to consciousness was partly experiential and partly the result of double ignorance. We do have some direct evidence of the baffling, magical potency of mind: through an unascertainable mechanism, consciousness appears able to make the world do its bidding from time to time. I want to raise my hand and, lo, the arm goes up, giving me the warm satisfaction of thinking that my mind is in control. But such experiences, unless subjected to a deeper scrutiny, contribute little to our understanding of the mind. In fact, they support continuing ignorance by conveying a sense of intimacy with what the mind is and what consciousness can do. This nescience guised by familiarity, when combined with primitive ignorance of physical process, make the temptation to seek mentalistic explanations of natural phenomena irresistible.

Mind on the Retreat

The dishonor that befell mind in the last hundred years is due in no small measure to disappointed expectations. For we thought not only that mental acts explained the occurrence of physical events, but also that this is something only they could do. The development of physical science disabused us of this fallacy by providing fruitful explanations of ever wider areas of physical fact. The history of modern science is at once the history of the gradual disappearance of mind as an explanatory principle. By the seventeenth century, we had a physics capable of accounting for the movement of inanimate matter without any reference to purposes. By the latter part of the nineteenth century, vital forces and entelechies were found to be unnecessary postulates in biology. In the last sixty years, subjective mind and private feeling have been banished from psychology. Computers can now reproduce all the higher cognitive functions of the mind and thereby attest that the hypothesis of mental causation is superfluous even when it comes to accounting for characteristically mental or conscious activities.

Some philosophers, such as Bergson, fought a rearguard action against what they thought was a reductionist and mechanistic science. The friends of science retaliated by denying the existence of consciousness altogether: many of them were (and still are) convinced that whatever has no place in the explanatory scheme of an ideally complete system of knowledge can have no reality at all. Scientists, who tend to be more cautious in interpreting their results than philosophers, usually avoid such metaphysical manifestos. But even they maintain that as a matter of sound scientific methodology, all reference to private consciousness and subjective mental acts must be eschewed.

Santayana is keenly aware of the success of science in dispensing with mind. He is also conscious of the devastating defeat in England, in the 1870s, of the clerics who fought the latest results of biology by quoting the Bible. He is convinced that physical explanation is, at least potentially, adequate to physical fact and that only science is qualified to explore the involutions of the material world. Apart from reaffirming the deep and inexplicable mystery of there being any existence at all, Santayana thinks that philosophers should be content with whatever knowledge of nature science can provide. The role of philosophy and religion is moral: it is to foster the life of reason and the spiritual life, instead of supposing themselves oracles that compete with science in furnishing empirical information.

This meek readiness to cede the physical world to science has an offsetting bold and positive result. If the sciences deal with all and only the facts of nature, the humanities retain control over its values. Empirical inquiry examines causes and means; only philosophical study and spiritual discipline are adequate to the appreciation of ultimate worth and ends. It is not, of course, that science finds it impossible to get at spirituality through its causes, for the source of everything is material. But since consciousness has an impenetrable skin, its internal logic, the song of its private life, remains its own and inviolate. Historically, we can view Santayana's philosophy as the final compromise between science and religion, the claims of an all-inclusive world of material objects and the tender call of the human heart. Santayana himself is inclined to think that his position represents no compromise at all, only the long overdue self-understanding of consciousness. However this may be, it is clear that objectivist science has unmatched institutional momentum and explanatory promise today. This means that the alternative, in our theories, to an impotent mind is none at all. In the light of our knowledge of neurophysiology, no view advocating the physical agency of immaterial awareness can command assent; if Santayana's epiphenomenalism is unacceptable, only a radical materialism without subjectivity is left.

Consciousness Impotent

In the long history of human thought, no philosopher can match Santayana in affirming the impotence of mind. He is steadfast throughout his career in wanting to disjoin belief in the existence of consciousness from confidence in its power. We have ample evidence, he thinks, not only of the existence of mind, but also of its radical distinction from the body. For consciousness is the light without which even the denial of its existence could not be entertained; it is a condition of all cognition. And its difference from everything physical should be evident to anyone reflecting on its privacy, nonspatiality, and syntheti-cally cognitive nature. We may well agree with all of this and yet find Santayana's view of the relation of body and mind difficult to accept. The great stumbling block is the apparent asymmetry or lack of mu-tuality between the partners: while the psyche displays life, power, and intelligence, spirit seems to have little to offer.

The asymmetry is not only apparent. Epiphenomenalism is the view that all conscious acts are brought into existence by events in the body and that none of them has an effect on itself, on other mental acts, or on the physical world. What, then, does consciousness *do*? Nothing; its sole function is to *be*. In being, it constitutes vistas of reality: it is the grasp of essence, truth, and the physical world. If our only interest is in causal processes, mind will seem an insignificant and useless at-tendant of material facts. This is the source of the bothersome disparity between body and mind: when it comes to generative force, matter has it all and mind makes no contribution. But there is another perspective to consider, which shows things in an altogether different light.

Matter Lacks Intrinsic Value

If the friends of matter view spirit as useless, the friends of spirit can retaliate by pronouncing matter worthless. In the strict sense, mat-ter is just that: its blind and ceaseless movement leaves it without anything of intrinsic worth. It is a huge engine of transactions which achieves all manner of things, but enjoys nothing. It may appear to aim at ends, but such ends, so long as they are bereft of feeling, con-stitute only temporary resting places in the flux. Only what is con-sciously enjoyed has intrinsic value; the useful acquires what modicum of goodness it has by its tendency to promote whatever is good in itself. No physical object is desired for its own sake; if it is not its use we want, then it is its possession. And no one in his right mind would want to own things without knowing it. We rest in the glee of pro-prietorship, not in legal title or grim physical embrace.

Just as from the standpoint of causation spirit is pure consequence, so if we focus on values, matter is all preliminaries. There is no causal force in mind, but there is no native value in matter. Matter makes mind possible, but it is only consciousness that redeems the dark rest-lessness of the flux. Power and value reside in different realms, and each views the other with disdain: for power the good is superfluous, for the soul matter is a snare. The reconciliation of force and feeling is one of the prime conditions of a rich human life. The location of the two in separate realms has profound implications for traditional theology.[1]

Spirit the Actuality of the Body

The two aspects of the relation of psyche and spirit require two conceptual frameworks to articulate them. On the generative side, we can employ the language of causation. Although this may not carry us far in understanding how the immaterial can arise from physical events, it is important to remember that, for Santayana, this bafflement is no greater than that appropriate at the fresh existence of anything. For help in explicating the relation from the standpoint of values, Santayana again turns to the Aristotelian categories he employed before. He conceives of the psyche as the potentiality of the mind and of consciousness as the fulfillment of the body's work. According to this view, the psyche exists for the sake of spirit: it is the development of consciousness that crowns its moral career. But this moral achievement is at once natural, for it follows upon the full actualization of its powers.

In the language we explored before, the life of the psyche is one of ceaseless process while spirit enjoys self-complete activities. This at once explains the absence of intrinsic values on the physical side: each process is restless motion towards an unstable terminus. In it means and end never coincide, and nothing done is, by itself, satisfactory. Activities, by contrast, are perfect and satisfactory achievements, performances in which means and ends cannot be split apart. Each activity thus carries its own end, its private, inalienable value, within itself. Santayana makes only one significant, modernizing change on Aristotle: he thinks of all activity as conscious. If the glow of feeling does not suffuse it, nothing can truly be an end. In the dark, insensitive material world, events are intrinsically temporal; none of these bursts through to the eternal actuality of a perfect act. It is the synthetic nature of such acts that raises them above the temporal flow and endows them, concomitantly, with their cognitive properties.

No Purposiveness

Santayana's repeated references to the blind irrationality of existence suggest that he does not believe purposes control material reality. Since

there is no God, there are no cosmic plans matter and history help
bring to pass. The conscious intentions of humans and animals are
impotent: they can neither cause nor even guide the processes of existence. And the physically real itself is piecemeal, consecutive, and im-
mune to the lure of values; the future and the nonexistent, no matter
how fine they would be if only they could charm themselves into existence, can exercise no influence over its present operations.

Our supposition that existence aims at ends is due to the mistaken
projection of values on the flux. We note the successive actualization
of certain tropes leading to what we think are desirable results. The
complexity of the trope and the apparent laboriousness of its actualization suggest a steadfast pursuit of the good. To literary psychology,
the desultory art of imagining the feelings of others, nature appears to
sigh with relief when the end is attained and to cling tenaciously to
whatever it achieves.

This, of course, is a matter of appearances only. Physical processes
shade into one another and have ends neither in the sense of aims nor
in the sense of definite terminations. What is the natural end of run-
ning water? Does wheat rust aim to grow and multiply in blissful
innocence or villainously to destroy the crops? Is the perfection of the
oyster in watery isolation or in a fine dish with spinach in New Orle-
ans? The supposed goals of natural events are conventionally chosen;
in themselves, they are but phases in the continuous process of the
world. Since we delight in seeing conscious intentions everywhere, we
convert eventual outcomes into antecedent powers and suppose that
whatever matter creates must have been the wellspring and inspiration
of its labors. Such anthropomorphism has its value; but it makes only
for good stories, not for good physics.

None of the above discussion implies, of course, that there is no
physical analogue to goal-seeking activity in the world. Complex organisms, and now even complicated machines, are capable of intricate
behavioral feats. Negative feedback loops enable robots and thermo-
stats to maintain a level of performance or a specifiable condition as if
they aimed at it. But the explanation of such remarkable achievements
requires no reference to anything future, mental, or nonexistent. Cleverly interconnected and thoroughly material sensory and control processes are adequate to sustain embodied intelligence. Living creatures,
from the paramecium to the paramedic, generate appropriate and variable responses to stimuli, maintain internal equilibrium, and obtain
the necessities of life. The human psyche, perhaps more than any other

being, displays physical goal-directed activity; Santayana thinks that, from the standpoint of its foundation, the entire structure of human values depends on such guided impulses. But the critical point is that intelligent behavior involves none of the three traditional forms of teleology; it requires no divine purposes, conscious plans, or natural but not-as-yet-existent goods to magnetize us.

Human Nature

We now have before us the parameters of human nature. Although Santayana is no believer in fixed species, he does think that we can assert some very general truths about who we are. All humans are compounds of body and mind. On the material side, we are struggling, needful, relatively intelligent psyches whose directed energies generate their values and whose activities can shape for a time some small part of the world. As spirits, we are either mock-participants in the cosmic dance, an audience nervously mimicking the concerns and blows and victories of the real agents, or else we are pure spectators without interest in the outcome of life. The body is mortal and will soon be gone. Consciousness will disappear with it, but can in the meantime transcend the cares of the world and establish some moments of spiritual freedom and intrinsic value. The psyche, if it acquires sufficient mastery over itself and the environment, can at best lead the life of reason before old age or the forces of the world cast it in the grave.

Apart from such generalities, not much can be said about human nature. No specific and universally valid prescriptions can be given as to how we are to order our lives, what we ought to do, what we should prefer. In a sense so general that it approaches an empty formula, the good life is the same for all of us. It is the actualization of our potential, the satisfaction of our nature or, as Santayana sometimes phrases it, the discharge of what is latent in us. But the details of the good life—and every life is just a collection of details—are determined by our individual constitutions and, though in a broad and loose sense all of us are human, we can differ from each other in significant ways. The dissimilarities are due to both nature and nurture. Biological endowments, social conditions, environmental influences, and psychological dispositions all conspire to make us the unique individuals we are. Some may suppose that our differences are paltry by comparison with our similarities. Yet they are real, and both the way values are generated and the nature of morality tend to magnify them.

How Values Arise

The material world displays no values and spirit in its purity is devoted to the disinterested contemplation of essence. Values arise only when matter and spirit work in harmony. The physical source and counterpart of value is what Santayana calls "impulse." His choice of this word is calculated to minimize the use of "desire," which carries connotations of consciousness. Impulse is a charge of energy directed upon some thing or state of affairs; it is stilled when its object is attained. When an impulse of the psyche targets some object, spirit comes to view it as suffused by the good. Santayana endorses G. E. Moore's idea that goodness is a simple, unanalyzable quality, even though he finds the rest of Moore's position, that goodness attaches to objects necessarily and for no assignable reason, preposterous.[2] Goodness, accordingly, is a simple essence of the sort that can be intuited but never embodied and which, when evoked, bathes actual or possible situations in a favorable light.

There is, then, a perfectly clear reason why values qualify certain actions and objects, and not others. Anything and anyone we view as good stands in a certain relation to our psyche. There are four terms in the complex value relationship: a material impulse, some object it fastens on, the essence good, and the conscious act that intuits it projected on the object. This view is an ontologically sophisticated version of the age-old position which holds that we do not desire things because they are good but, rather, they are good because we desire them. It has been criticized not only on the ground that it relativizes values, but also on account of the promiscuity of goods it generates. For if this view is correct, there are no objective, eternal, and absolute values. And anything anyone desires, no matter how petty, foul, or harmful, will in fact be good.

No Absolute Values

Santayana gladly endorses both of the consequences that have been thought fatal to the view. That there are no timeless and independent values is the beginning of secular wisdom in his eyes. And the goodness of the loathsome, if it is truly desired, has the status of simple, obvious fact. But, it might be objected, such things are good only to the person who wants them. Of course, Santayana replies, and the same is true of everything that is good. This, however, might be taken to imply that there is no distinction between the real good and what in a thoughtless moment anyone might prize. Santayana rejects the implication; his reasons for doing so are complex and take us to the heart of his moral philosophy.

Although the good is not an objective standard of existence and behavior, it is independent of what we think. Its relational quality ties it to our nature and impulses, not to stray opinions. There are any number of things I might abstractly think excellent; unless I have a living interest in them, however, they will not be seen, embraced, and acted on as goods. Moralists should be familiar with this phenomenon: it is our relation to many of their highest precepts. This still leaves a very large number of goods each of us desires, and some of these are trivial, some destructive, and some incompatible. By itself, each is nevertheless a genuine value to the person desiring it and under his or her circumstances; if it cannot be attained or retained, it will be mourned as perhaps a small but real loss.

The Life of Reason

The moral life consists in bringing order to this proliferation of impulses. Kant was right in believing that morality inevitably involves the suppression of desires. But we must eliminate yearnings not in the name of stern duty but on behalf of the rational maximization of satisfactions. The suppression of desires, therefore, should never be wholesale; it should take the form only of trimming their luxuriance so that the largest possible number of them may be fulfilled. The ideal of such maximal satisfaction is what Santayana calls "the life of reason." In this life, we desire and work for the consummation of the largest compatible set of our impulses.

In the history of philosophy, reason has frequently been conceived as an other-worldly force, a divine stranger that brings enlightenment and justice. As such, it is usually opposed not only to the transitory world and our uncertain beliefs, but also to the bias of our passionate attachments. The problem of high-minded thinkers who champion the view is that few humans find this guileless guest in themselves and fewer yet can see it as their true self. And not even contorted logic will explain whence the visitor came and why, in the face of disregard and disappointment, it remains our long-suffering boarder instead of returning to its sunnier home.

The philosophy of animal faith offers no myths about untarnished or transcendental strangers. Reason, for it, must be intelligence in action. If it is to have any effect on our daily lives, it must be of the same nature as the passions that define our behavior. Accordingly, Santayana maintains that reason itself is an animal impulse, albeit a very special one.[3] What makes it extraordinary is that it is not directed on things, activities, or states of affairs; its object is the order or harmony of other impulses. It is a second-level desire perhaps unique to humans, for it involves a high level of intelligence: its operation requires taking the future into account in order to decide when present satisfactions may have to be sacrificed to the long-range good.

Rational Maximization of Satisfactions

Reason, the formal impulse for harmony, is an advocate of animal desires. Its aim is to select and support impulses on the basis of their strength, fulfillability, and compatibility. The energy of a desire is usually proportionate to the intensity of the satisfaction it can provide: neither as desire nor from the standpoint of its fulfillment is a mild craving for ice cream a match for the burning passion we might have for our mates. The possibility of gratifying our desires is a crucial feature of rational living. Wanting things our greatest exertions could not secure leaves us frustrated and with a sense of missed opportunities.

What we call the compatibility of impulses is really the compatibility of their satisfactions. All of us know how easy it is to entertain a collection of absurd desires. There is no problem in *their* coexistence; it is only the fulfillment of one that excludes the gratification of the others. From the standpoint of reason, the compatibility of desires (or of their satisfactions) is their most important property and the most difficult to judge. Its simplest form is temporal impossibility: I cannot both entertain my wife in luscious privacy and host a beer party on a Sunday afternoon. Irreconcilability is the fundamental issue in the conflict of short-term and long-term goods: such desires for immediate gratification as drinking heavily and then driving home are not likely to be harmonious with remaining physically whole or staying out of jail which, presumably, are more established cravings. The question of the life-sustaining or life-endangering quality of desires and satisfactions itself comes to no more than an issue of consistency, for the incompatibility of an impulse (such as to slash one's wrists) with life is simply its incompatibility with our desires for what life can provide. In its most general application, the impossibility of joint satisfaction explains the important idea of cost: all the things we want but cannot have if we act on a given desire are the price we have to pay for the good it yields.

The Real and the Apparent Good

We can now see that Santayana is keenly conscious of the distinction between the "real" and a merely momentary good. The difference is not that the short-term good is not good, after all. It is, rather, that the real good of any individual is a system of fulfillable desires and intense, compatible satisfactions. Stray desires and immediate gratifications must be measured by how they mesh with the system; if they are judged unworthy of our efforts, it is because their cost is too high. They are rejected not because they are bad, but on the ground that, though good, they are not as good as what they would make impossible.

The life of reason is, therefore, a sane existence of harmonized desires. Personal and civic virtues find a place in it to the extent they are compatible with, or required by, our other satisfactions. This places them on a par with every other proposed mode of conduct. Their propriety derives not from their intrinsic nature, but from the central role they play in our harmonious system of desires. Sound personal habits and generous sociality tend to enhance the satisfactions possible to us; this and this alone is the source of the moral force they bear. And it is important to remember that the contribution they make to our good life is contingent on our condition. If we could grow, like the oak tree, without social aid, if, as is said of Lucifer, dissolute habits did not sap our life, virtues would be a useless luxury. And if we prize neither order and sociality, nor what they make possible, such as a longer, peaceful life, they will have no significant value in our eyes. Combative people, drug addicts, and social suicides may all fall in this category; we cannot say they fail to lead the good life because they love a good we cannot comprehend.

The Life of Reason Has No Universal Content

This reveals two central traits of the life of reason. Though calling it a life of harmonized desires appears to confer uniformity on it, the diversity of impulses and impulse-systems makes it in its concrete form a collection of very different lives. To speak of lives as governed by reason, therefore, is not to attribute any specific content or values to them. They share only the formal or general feature of the drive for harmony, the intelligent maximization of satisfactions. This implies a measure of reflection, self-knowledge, and control, but such qualities themselves presuppose an already existing structure of desires and tendencies. The person devoted to reason can, thus, never be recognized by what he values or by what she does; only by comparing the totality of an individual's impulses with those he or she chooses to actualize could we determine whether reason is an active power in that life. Since this is difficult or impossible to do and anything less would represent a hasty and external assessment, Santayana urges that we restrain our readiness to judge others and remain skeptical of the judgments we must make. In any case, the fact that two people lead widely divergent lives is no evidence that one lives better or is more rational than the other; it may well be that reason graces their existence to an equal extent, but the initial fund of their impulses renders them different.

I have now shown that the life of reason lacks universal content. A second remarkable trait it displays is that it can be led only by individuals. No society has an organic body or a social mind. None, therefore, has impulses or desires of its own. Though societies consist of individuals, they are not themselves individuals of a larger, more important sort. Small physical objects can constitute larger ones, but a collection of psyches never makes for a vast organic whole such as some philosophers have supposed society or the state to be. And the unity and privacy of intuition make it impossible for spirits to be compounded into larger minds. Since reason is an organic impulse, it cannot serve as an active power in society. Because society has no impulses of its own to restrain, however, there is fortunately no need for such an immense, direct communal force. Whatever rationality society has derives from the rationalizing efforts of its members.

Radical Individualism

Santayana's individualism is radical and total. The social whole has no ontological status independent of that of its parts. It has no agency apart from the efficacy of its constituent psyches. It has no intelligence other than the light individual spirits provide. And it has no value distinct from the worth of the persons who are its members. This individualism is, for Santayana, not a political creed: it is an insight, based on his ontology, into the moral constitution of the world. Individuals are the ultimate source and bearers of all good, the center and fulcrum of the moral universe. The value of societies must be measured by the quality of psyches they help to create and the nature and variety of satisfactions they permit or promote. Political systems must be evaluated on the same principles. There is no one form of government superior to all the rest. The diversity of psyches and relativity of values penetrate to the heart of the social order: different social and political arrangements are appropriate to diverse persons with divergent impulses.

The fact that in its immediacy the life of reason is an individual affair does not negate the social conditioning of psyches. Although they are biological structures, their impulses can be shaped by social influences. The opportunities of satisfaction, many of which are created by community, arouse or redirect desires. Formal and informal education stamp young persons with the mark of their native tradition. Our social origins and shared fulfillments are writ large in our souls and many feel that without common customs and companionship life cannot be good. Santayana readily admits all of this. But, he reminds us, whatever forces shape our souls, when it comes to deciding what to do, each of us stands radically alone. In the end, the life of reason, like a spider's web, is spun out of our own substance by our own agency. The question then is not where our impulses come from but what to do with them. For the community cannot act on my behalf and never suffers my pain when I am wrong.

Individual Nature Determines the Good

We can now see why the generation of values and the nature of morality magnify the differences between individuals. Values are grounded in impulses and morality is the art of creating rich systems of satisfaction out of what we feel impelled to do. This implies that, for purposes of intelligent action and the good life, our individual natures include not only established biological and psychological traits, but also all the impulses of our animal life. "Individual nature" has two meanings here. It stands for the totality of structures, tendencies, and passions of which the psyche consists, all the tropes embodied in it at a time. But it also designates the being we are in process of making of ourselves, the psyche as it must be to lead the life of reason. In the first sense, "individual nature" is inclusive, in the second it is normative. But because they embrace specific desires and context-dependent goods, both senses stress the diversity between psyche and psyche. Santayana does not believe there is a difference in the world between essential and accidental features; as a result, each of us is everything he is. The more essential, systematic nature morality demands, though still inclusive of minor traits and cravings, is not born or given but achieved.

The good of each person is determined by his or her nature. This means that in attempting to create a satisfying life, we must work with whatever talents and desires we find in ourselves. Self-knowledge is important not because it yields insight into some essential self, but as a means to the honest inventory of our assets and liabilities. The critical skill in self-assessment is the ability to distinguish long-term from short-term desires and needs. It is only on the basis of our long-term interests and repeatable satisfactions that we can create a stable self and undertake the task of making life rational. Passing fancies and mindless passions fraught with risk are threats to a sensible existence; if they are not shunned, they may quickly pull down the carefully built edifice of sound habits and good human relations, and may in the end destroy life itself. It is not that the life of reason forbids all immediacy and passionate release. But whatever it permits must be at least not life-destructive, and it is best if they are harnessed to serve human purposes. In the life of reason, art, science, religion, even the purest works of mind are ends only as parts of a larger whole. They are expressive of who we are, and it is our use of them, the way we fit them in our world, that defines their meaning and their value.

Control

But knowledge is only one of the conditions of constructing a stable self. Two other indispensable requirements are control over self and mastery of materials. Without the power to restrain our urgent impulses, knowledge of long-term good would be in vain. Ability to delay or altogether resist the gratification of some desires is the foundation of civilization. And the rechanneling or sublimation of impulse serves as the one sure source of the arts. But control over self alone might well turn us into lonely Eastern mystics. The life of reason involves the satisfaction of desires, not their extirpation, and in a material world that is impossible without a measure of control over the generative order. Cooperative action, the useful arts, the technology science begets enable us to achieve at least some of our mundane purposes. Although Santayana is clear that control is never complete, the achievements of culture remain impermanent, and human life itself will certainly run out, he points with satisfaction to the rich and bright existence we can fashion in the flux and enjoy without regret for a brief moment.

Santayana's detailed account of the life of reason was developed around the turn of the century. Although in one of his private notebooks he remarks that he has been called many things but never an optimist, the tone of his earlier work, especially *The Life of Reason,* is positive and hopeful. The philosophical distance, the dwarfing perspective of infinity is always present in his thought, yet in these volumes he finds the Greek ideal of a measured and successful life not only possible but attractive. World War I was a traumatic, nearly disastrous, intellectual and moral experience for Santayana's confident generation. He himself saw a world ostensibly governed by reason collapse; this served only to confirm and nourish his native suspicion that we are irrational, that life is mad,[4] and that human effort is in the end all vain. Although he never repudiated the ideal of the life of reason, and it stands as the silent foundation of some elements in his later work, it nevertheless receded into the background. He came to view it as but one possible perfection, and it no longer held his interest. It was replaced at the center of his attention by the spiritual life. This change of concern is deeper than a change of values; it is a move, as we shall see, from an existence structured by values to the possibility of transcending animal partiality, and hence the notion of the good, altogether.

Incommensurable Goods

The person devoted to the life of reason looks inescapably like a cultured, urbane, and successful Westerner. Can we suppose that we represent the crowning moral achievement of the universe? A more provincial thinker than Santayana might well rub his hands with glee at this idea and present himself and a few friends as models for the world to imitate. Santayana easily avoids this snare, which even such an intelligent and generous supporter of diversity as J. S. Mill was unable to escape. What shall we say of those who show no interest in a harmony of desires and gladly fall hostage to a splendid passion? Nothing derogatory. Reason is an optional desire. Those who have it may be well served by it, but Achilles and his burly friends find restraint onerous and a long life boring. Are we better off than they? Certainly, from our own perspective, for we can sip wine and gaze into the evening long after their death. But that is certainly not their view: they pity us, even as they die, for never having felt a keen excitement, given with self-forgetful ease, or ridden the crest of passion's tidal wave.

Reason as a structuring impulse is not complusory. Those who have it may live longer than others, but not necessarily better. For the better and worse must be determined by reference to the internal nature of a life, its native ideals, not external standards. Different lives are thus essentially incommensurable. Their comparison occurs in the private imagination which, though an organ of sympathy, cannot escape the partiality of its source. It is not, of course, that moral failure is impossible: we can fall short of actualizing the best that is in us. But the best is relative to what our nature demands and our circumstances permit, and both nature and circumstances are variable and individual.

Substantial (rather than verbal) moral agreement and the possibility of evaluating people by uniform criteria presuppose at least a partial similarity of natures. Only the likeness of our wants and needs can justify community standards and a social order. Societies not based on the spontaneous harmony of like-natured individuals must sustain themselves by the imposition of norms alien to many of their members. Such militancy toward neighbors and outsiders, though widespread and understandable, represents a major moral evil. It interferes with the natural processes of free self-actualization and makes the achievement of satisfaction and moral identity impossible.

Toleration

The contrasting, apparently universal, moral good is toleration. Plato thought that justice was a matter of minding one's own business, fulfilling one's function, without meddlesome intervention in the affairs of others. But this was a prescription for docility not tolerance, for it ceded the formulation of rules and the assignment of functions to a small minority of the presumably wise. Toleration is a more positive virtue: it is appreciation of the autonomy of others and cordial wishes for their odd success. If we are tolerant, we respect persons not authority, for we then refuse to believe that government, or even we ourselves, know the good of another better than she can know it herself. A person who never raises doubts about himself is the most dangerous of dogmatists; toleration, by contrast, grows in the soil of skepticism about one's own discernment and generosity in seeing the equal legitimacy of alien goods.

If we are tolerant, we accept the right of others to seek their own fulfillment and welcome their acts with distant sympathy. This attitude is easiest to take to people at a safe interval from us in time or space, whose habits and actions make little difference to what we want. But what if the fulfillment of another's desire strips me of what I hold most precious? The world is full of robbers and rapists and murderers whose pursuit of their art is not casual; shall we tolerate their misbehavior so long as it is truly necessary for their self-expression? In cases of conflict when all goods cannot prevail, are we justified if we prefer one and subdue the others? Can tolerance be a strategy for life in the realm of matter where struggle is the norm? Is universal toleration the groundwork of a morality or of a paralysis that stops all action out of sympathy? Without answering these questions, Santayana's ethical theory can be neither convincing nor complete.

Chapter Six

The Spiritual Life

Schopenhauer on the Saintly Life

Judging by his writings, though not perhaps by his personal life, no philosopher has ever had a keener appreciation of the legitimacy of all competing claims than Arthur Schopenhauer. But for Schopenhauer sympathy led to moral paralysis. If every desire is equally legitimate, I have no moral justification for resisting aggression. In cases of conflict only the immoral can act: those who understand the innocent urgency of every impulse, those who respect the will of everyone must not do anything to deny to others what they need or want. In this way, universal sympathy becomes primarily the love of alien goods; one's own desires begin to feel odious and altruism appears to demand self-sacrifice. The idea that everything is of equal value, moreover, is only one step away from the thought of the worthlessness of it all. Schopenhauer ends with the devastating conclusion that effort is futile and life unjustified. The only moral and rational course is to move beyond all desires to a state of changeless indifference, a saintly transcendence of concern for self and world.

This chilling view invites comparison with Santayana on two counts. First, Schopenhauer thinks that the relativity of values requires universal toleration, which inevitably ends in moral paralysis. And, second, he maintains that there is no possibility of human fulfillment in the world of action; our only escape is to overcome body and will in a sort of spirituality. Santayana flirts with both of these positions. His final opinions are understood best by exploring why he rejects and how he modifies Schopenhauer's cosmic pessimism.

Is the Good of Others Higher than Mine?

A full understanding of the equal legitimacy of divergent value structures commits us to the toleration, even if not to the appreciation, of alien goods. But, properly conceived, this toleration is not without

104

limit. For if all systems of preference are alike in being internally justified and externally incommensurable, my reasonable needs and claims cannot be disregarded. They are as legitimate as anybody else's, so I can have no obligation to surrender them in order that another may thrive. The demand for self-sacrifice presupposes, in fact, that the good of others rate higher than mine: it is only by reference to this greater value that I can be asked to relinquish my desires or my life.

If everyone is on an equal plane, each is entitled to pursue her activities and to seek his happiness. The greatest good comes about when the satisfaction of one does not require the defeat or destruction of others. But when conflict is unavoidable, there is no moral requirement that anyone back down. Each can, and from his own standpoint should, stand firm on principle, persist in his ideas, and protect his interests. The result is likely to be significant moral loss: the ensuing struggle will probably destroy some people or at least their hopes. Yet in such cases the damage is due not to the perversity of self-defense but to the structure of the human world, in which conflicting goods are commonplace. And it is important to remember that since true loss is loss of principle and hence of self, the moral harm would be the same even if we gave in without a fight.

This tragic view of conflict is best expressed in the terms with which it has become associated in the history of thought. Our desires, actions, and beliefs are natural expressions of who we are, and we are ourselves by a pervasive but innocent necessity. The necessity is, of course, not logical: a world in which we or others are different is conceivable without contradiction. Yet once we are weighted by a nature, we must be who we are and we must do what the inner person in us demands. Just as the spider is impelled to weave its web, we must spin involuted lives out of our substance. The process is natural and difficult to reverse; its internal logic and momentum carry us past the doubts and hesitations of a fearful mind. The primary moral task is to achieve wholeness by acting out who we are. This uncompromising commitment to the life and truth in us does not make us condemn what others perpetrate. We try to understand who they are and accept without complaint what they do. But when they threaten what is dear to us, neither understanding nor sympathy can stand in the way of what *we* must do in its defense.

Using this language of self-realization makes it clear that the tolerant person is not without moral justification in defending himself against aggression. And the aggressor is surely vindicated from his own perspective. The only thing lacking is an overarching system of values in terms of which the two justifications could be compared and assessed. Yet what would such a single, cosmic scheme of good avail us? It would yield only added self-assurance that in our battles God is on our side. The idea of an ultimate moral adjudication makes conflict fanatical: instead of reducing the impulse to fight, it incites glorious, undying antagonisms.

A Sane Pluralism of Values

Santayana's view that values are relative to the nature and needs of individuals can be seen, in this way, to restore sanity to the moral world. Only when we shed the disagreeable tendency to pronounce universal judgment on all manner of things and learn that there is no justification for imposing our will on others, can we attend to the real work of morality, which is the harmonious development of self and the tolerant, even helpful, embrace of our fellows. Such toleration is consistent with self-defense. Although the conflict of values is lamentable and inevitably leads to the destruction of some good, it is an inescapable feature of reality. To his immense credit, Santayana always rejects cheap comfort: he systematically refuses to endorse the romantic belief that, through all the changes of a tortured world, everything worthwhile is somehow forever preserved. The philosophy of animal faith can never deny our organic origins and our animal fate.

The tolerant pluralism Santayana's moral theory entails is thoroughly American in tone. It is founded in respect for persons and a strong distaste for interfering in their affairs. Although Santayana does not dwell on autonomy in his writings, he showed a keen sense for it in his treatment of people and in his personal life. He was careful to let others, even those (such as his secretary, Cory) who were dependent on him, make their own decisions, and insisted on the same right for himself. This commendable readiness to have each of us lead his or her own life may well have been the source of Bertrand Russell's distorted assessment of him as "aloof and contemptuous."[1] How naturally such esteem for individual choice goes with warmth and generosity is aptly illustrated by the fact that, in one of his periods of intense financial need, Russell himself had been the recipient of a large anonymous gift from his supposedly cold and distant friend.

Traditional Views of Contemplation

There is a tradition in Western thought that views the moral life as of great but not ultimate significance. Aristotle, an early and eloquent spokesman of this view, thought that nothing requiring physical action can serve as the best and most fulfilling activity for human beings. Our greatest perfection is possible only if we manage to transcend time and instrumentality altogether: we accomplish this in the godlike contemplation of eternal things. Thought, therefore, and not action crowns human existence, and the highest thought must not seek or investigate truth but possess and enjoy it.

The proper objects of such contemplation were supposed by various thinkers to be eternal or changeless things, timeless truths, aesthetic objects, and God. The contemplative act itself was conceived in ways as diverse as pure intellection, aesthetic enjoyment, and mystical union. But there was always substantial agreement within the tradition concerning the timeless ultimacy of the objects of contemplation, the immediacy of the contact between us and these objects, and the belief that only such self-complete activities can constitute the final fruit of human life.

Santayana's theory of the spiritual life clearly belongs in this family of views. The close similarity between the spiritual life and traditional ideas of intellectual virtue will become evident in the discussions that follow. But before we look at the resemblances, it is important to note a crucial difference. Proponents of contemplation, spirituality, and the mystical life typically think of their favored activity as the highest attainment of mankind. As such, it is supposed to represent an ideal we all aim, or ought to aim, at achieving. Yet Santayana's moral relativism makes it impossible for him to embrace this view. Excellent as spirituality may seem to those devoted to it, it is not a universal good. Football players, politicians, and the owners of sleazy motels may not value it at all, and it is simply impossible to tell such people that their priorities are disarranged. The spiritual life is thus an optional perfection: for those whose nature predisposes them to the quiet enjoyment of the immediate, it is the finest and freest human act. Those who prefer the challenges and bustle of life in the flux, on the other hand, find it pallid and weary. If each view truthfully expresses the demands of a nature, neither one is wrong. Spirituality is the proper fulfillment of some lives and an object of ridicule in others.

Intuition and Intent

Santayana's view of the spiritual life is widely misunderstood. One reason for this is that the very notion of spirituality seems alien, if not unintelligible, to many of us today. And it is not at all easy to see how spirituality, especially in Santayana's sense of the term, could constitute a *life*. Getting clear on these two issues should go a long way toward developing a proper grasp of Santayana's ideas about the liberation of consciousness.

In discussing the mind-body problem I noted that what Santayana calls "spirit" is simply what we normally mean by the word "consciousness." This cognitive light falls on essences and the natural world alike. In its simplest form it is an act of awareness that enters into cognitive contact with some essence. So long as there is no attempt to transcend the immediate through the belief that such an essence reveals the presence or nature of an existent, the intuition is pure. In pure intuition we rest in the contemplation or enjoyment of the intrinsic features of whatever is immediately presented.

Since we are animals, however, intuition is rarely pure. The demands of practical life make us take the essences in consciousness as signs of external things: our interest is in learning the disposition of the world around us, instead of enjoying the lovely sights and sounds it provides. Animal faith in the form of intent, the urge to look for meaning in sensory phenomena, makes us overlook the aesthetic qualities of the immediate in favor of the causal properties of the physical objects they presumably reveal.

The practical interest that structures ordinary consciousness keeps our minds subservient to animal need. The cruel irony is that since mind has no physical power, its devotion to advancing the body's good is totally without effect. The bondage of consciousness to animal life is, therefore, the source of immense unnecessary distress and distraction. Although the mind greets the success of its organ with delight, the bulk of its existence is taken up with the concern, frustration, and pain that constitute the primary way in which sustained organic struggle rises to consciousness.

Pure Intuition Spiritual

The proper role of intuition is not to reflect animal toil, but simply to scan the immediate. Animal faith, the powerful impulse to take essences as the signs of surrounding substance, removes the possibility of pure intuition and converts the mind into an organ of inquiry and belief. Such urge to believe is alien to consciousness in its purity; if spirit were not harnessed in the service of animal life, it would be spiritual. To say that consciousness is spiritual in this sense means simply that it shows the proper nature of spirit: it takes pleasure in whatever is present instead of seeking or exploring the absent.

We can see, then, that Santayana's account of spirituality strips it of its otherworldliness. Although it involves a transcendence of the animal in us, this is accomplished not by passing the limits of the empirical but by stopping before its portals. The spiritual is what rests in the immediate and seeks nothing beyond; it is consciousness savoring the self-identity of whatever essence is presented for as long as the appearance endures. Epistemically it is free of belief and morally it is without longing. It is pleased with what it receives, yet feels no regret when the essence before it disappears. As Santayana expresses it beautifully in his autobiography, pure consciousness has the world as its host and it is not a reluctant guest: it happily witnesses the parade of forms nature provides. But it is also a guest with exemplary manners: it never asks for seconds at the feast and shows no reluctance when it is time to leave.

Spirituality Free of Values

The central feature of spirituality is that it shows neither preference nor aversion. It involves an indifference to fate, a neutrality with respect to what will or what should be. The internal tone of its intuitions is, of course, anything but indifferent: a free joyousness pervades each moment of the spiritual life. But in its relations to both essence and existence, a pure spirit makes no choices: peaceful acquiescence characterizes its attitude toward its objects and even its own continued existence. In this way, it frees itself from morality. The transcendence is not in the name of some higher good that can be achieved only by rejecting conventional values. Since the source of the good is animal preference, this is a liberation from all values and all partiality. Its organ, of course, continues to impose grotesque perspectives on spirit and to provide for it an odd selection of objects: this is a proper and incontestable sign of finite, animal origins. But spirit does not embrace any one vista in preference to others. And if it is truly spiritual, it does not protest or reject any either, but simply accepts each for what it is: one essence out of an infinity it could contemplate.

Another way to make this point is to say that the proper object of pure intuition is always an essence. The essences are grasped and enjoyed for their intrinsic, formal features, not for any extrinsic relation in which they might stand to existing things or to the self. With respect to their purely formal characteristics, all essences are on a par: each is a changeless universal eternally identical with itself. There is, then, no way to choose between them viewed as forms only: none is more suitable for contemplation than any other. Selection of the essence we intuit and the activity in which we engage is the work of the psyche whose life requires to be protected and sustained. Pure intuition, on the other hand, is the intellectual counterpart of the realm of essence; it is the impartial readiness to conceive or to grow conscious of anything. The realm of essence offers no basis for preferring one of its members to any others, and pure intuition has no principle of choice of its own to contribute. The result is that in its spiritual phase consciousness experiences a "disintoxication"[2] from values, which is simply a liberation from the concerns of animal life.

Pure Intuition as Activity

Consciousness can, of course, never escape its organic origin. Since it consists of intuitions each of which has to be generated individually and each of which lapses before long, even its spiritual phase presupposes the continued operation of a psyche. But viewed internally or from the standpoint of how spirituality is experienced, we can find only intuited essences and nothing existent or organic. Pure intuition is the finest form of activity in the Aristotelian sense of this term: in it there is no distinction between past, present, and future, and none between means and end. It is a condition in which time appears to stand still and which is instrumental to the achievement of nothing beyond itself. When it occurs, it is enjoyed for its own sake, as an end in itself. Its presence shatters the unbroken cycle of means and ends of which animal life consists, and gives us a taste of the joy freedom from toil allows.

This conception of the spiritual life appears to be close to Schopenhauer's account of saintliness. There is indeed agreement that ultimate perfection is incompatible with devotion to values and the exercise of will. It requires, moreover, in the opinion of both thinkers, indifference to fate and a transcendence of the self. But here the similarity ends. For Schopenhauer views spirituality as destructive of existence, while Santayana sees it as possible only so long as the body thrives. Schopenhauer thinks it can be achieved only by torturous effort, while Santayana conceives of it as a natural perfection. Schopenhauer maintains that it is the only possible escape from misery, while Santayana holds that it is a satisfying but optional fruit of certain forms of life. And Schopenhauer declares that it resembles the dark unconsciousness of nirvana, while Santayana asserts that it is all joyousness and light.

The central difference between these two philosophers is that Schopenhauer thinks of saintliness as an alternative to life, whereas Santayana's spirituality is an enriching dimension of it. Here again, Santayana's respect for common sense stands in bold relief: he views it as the accumulated wisdom of the human race. Only an ill or ill-humored person could think that there is nothing to life but misery and that the function of transcendence is to end it all. It is to Santayana's great credit that he recognizes the possibility of a spiritual life even in the midst of business and that he conceives of it as a natural activity in which human beings may at any time engage. Whitecaps are not alternatives to waves but parts of them and native to the sea.

Santayana's notion of spirituality carries additional attractiveness because of the way it combines the intellectual, aesthetic, and mystical elements in its tradition. Since the spiritual life is a form of consciousness, its nature is cognitive. Each moment of it consists of an awareness of essence, and all awareness is intelligent grasp. This apprehension is focused on forms that are directly seized and instantly enjoyed. The immediacy, intimacy, and delight of this union are all aesthetic features of it. Since intuition is private and the essences that serve as its objects are simply what they are, the content of spirituality is as incommunicable as a mystic vision. Language cannot capture the flavor of the immediate and judgments that attach alien predicates to an essence falsify its self-identity. Though my pure intuitions are clarity and light themselves to me, they remain hidden and ineffable events for everyone else.

Spiritual Life and the Life of Reason

At this point the second question, that of how spirituality can constitute an existence, must inevitably arise. Santayana speaks of the spiritual *life,* and some commentators contrast this with the life of reason.

If both are life-patterns, they are likely to be incompatible. Santayana himself admits that they "pull in different ways": reason strives for the maximization of satisfactions, spirit has no desires and no values, and aims at nothing at all. If the spiritual life is an alternative to the life of reason, it is sure to be a poor second from the physical point of view. A life that expends no effort in satisfying needs and pays no heed to substance and to danger can only stumble, suffer, and then quickly pass on. Could Santayana have meant that one's spiritual "life" is but the last days of one's unconcern after animal bias is renounced?

The answer is clearly no. He emphatically denies that there is op- position between spirit and reason: they are not in competition for a single prize. Reason is an impulse to structure a varied and lengthy life. Spirit, by contrast, is content to bloom in a timeless moment. Reason fosters and supports the psyche: one of the marks of its success is healthy physical life. Spirit profits by this health but leaves it un- helped and unhindered; its own achievement is measured by clarity of consciousness and steadiness of mind. If we think of reason as a gar- dener, the spiritual life is a flower tended. It is not the only flower in the garden of human achievements, but it is of special interest because nothing else does justice to the native propensity of consciousness.

Two Meanings of "Life"

The spiritual life, then, is not an alternative to ordinary or biological existence. It is, in fact, not a life in the same sense at all. There are two importantly different senses of "life," which both our materialist culture and, oddly, its "right-to-life" critics find difficult to distin- guish. In its broadest designation, "life" refers to the more or less uni- fied operation of an organism. In the case of humans, this involves some measure of bodily integrity, heart and lung function, and the coordinating activity of the lower brain. All of this is, in Santayana's language, the work of the psyche. It is organic process that requires no consciousness and frequently occurs without it.

There is also another sense in which we speak of life. We say "He leads the life of Riley" and do not mean that the poor Irishman's heart has been transplanted into his breast. And in such exclamations as "That's the life!" we clearly do not refer to optimal biological process. What we have in mind is an existence suffused with meaning and delight, a manner of being in which we can take satisfaction. Such existence is invariably conscious and enjoyable for what it is. Its organic ground is not denied, only overlooked in the intensity of blissful feeling. Life in this sense is the excitement of a party or our self-forgetful passion at a game. The relation of the first sense of "life" to the current one is well symbolized by the connection between heartbeat and the occasional stream of pleasure it makes possible. We may think of biological function as the root of human life, and of consciousness as its fruit. Or, in more current terms, we can say that organic processes establish the quantity of life, while conscious satisfaction measures its quality.

Spirit and Time

This latter way of drawing the contrast underscores the important fact that temporal duration is centrally tied to life in its first or biological sense, but not at all to life in the sense of fulfillment. Time-consciousness is largely incompatible with unfettered enjoyment. In fact, we find that the more we are aware of the passage of minutes and hours, the less we can let ourselves go to take pleasure in what they bring us. A single moment of self-forgetful, absorbing delight, by contrast, is felt as a timeless and perfect world. Time, at least for the subject, exists only in the interval between desire and fulfillment, means and end; when means and end are one and satisfaction is instantaneous, passage itself recedes and we live in an eternal now.

Spirituality constitutes a life only in this second sense: it is consciousness liberated from the instruments and worries of the world and concentrated in the present moment. As such, it neither needs nor has the duration and continuity of substantial, organic processes. It exists in the interstices of nature and flowers suddenly and intermittently at surprising times and places. It is a life because it is alive with the cognitive light of consciousness and with feeling that is playful and carefree. It is existence at its best, the pure actuality which is the body's song.

Spirituality, then, is not a style of life or a manner of being, but simply life itself when it reaches white heat. It occurs, like lightning, wherever the physical conditions for it are right, and its existence is always episodic, momentary, and fleeting. It can, of course, be fostered: by distancing ourselves from the forces we symbolize as the world, the flesh, and the devil, we can enhance the frequency of our pure intuitions.[3] But even here, there are limits. Since mind is a product of animal bodies, total liberation is impossible. A consciousness

completely free of organic attachments could not exist, and even a significant increase in spirituality may indicate a psyche that is turning
away from the tasks of animal life and hence becoming especially vulnerable to disease and decay.

Spirituality in Everyday Life

We can see, then, that Santayana's naturalistic philosophy of animal
faith serves as the framework and foundation even of his conception of
the spiritual life. For in addition to affirming the physical conditioning
of consciousness and denying the possibility of a completely spiritual
existence, he maintains that pure intuition can flourish in anyone and
even in the midst of ordinary practice. It is, in fact, within the parameters of everyday existence that the spiritual life belongs. For although
it can be achieved by averting our gaze from needs, agencies, and instruments in the material world, its most frequent occurrence is as a
"mental transcript" or conscious expression of mastery over these
instruments.

To understand this point, we need to remember that Aristotle
thought of delight as the unimpeded activity, of that which accompan-
ies the unimpeded activity, of an organ directed upon appropriate objects. Our eyes, for example, yield pleasure when they work well and
are used to observe beautiful things. This suggests the idea, confirmed
by experience, that perfectly executed complex organic processes, although physical, are normally accompanied by intrinsically delightful
moments of consciousness. The pleasure results not from reflection on
how well we do, but is a natural by-product of the process itself: it is
the completion or consummation of material events. The resulting intuitions are, like precious beads, whole and valuable in and of themselves. They constitute spirituality in the midst of business and are in
no way inferior to the achievements of dry holy men.

Absorption in the Immediate

The spiritual life, then, bursts in upon us whenever we become absorbed in the immediate. The temporary liberation of consciousness
from belief in substance is adequate to focus it on the intrinsic features
of whatever essence is presented. This happens in sensory awareness
when sights and sounds are taken not as signs indicative of the presence
of external objects but simply as the sense-qualities they immediately

and manifestly are. To the hungry person, the smell of peeled apples may signify a pie. But it is also possible to concentrate on this magnificent fragrance in isolation from its source and promise. When we do this, we remove it from its natural but extraneous context and eliminate its meaning; it then stands revealed, and is enjoyed, for what it is. In its immediacy everything is a self-identical essence. As chemists well know, what we call the aroma of peeled apples has no intrinsic reference to knife or fruit; it just happens to be the essence we normally intuit when certain physical events occur. The same form can be evoked by substitute chemical means, and if we then take it to reveal what goes on in the kitchen, we are simply wrong. The point is, of course, to assign no cognitive significance to it at all: whenever we succeed in doing this, we have an essence in its purity and for a moment live the spiritual life.

Absorption in the immediate can take place on the conceptual no less than on a sensory plane. The only difference between the two is in the specific objects contemplated. But the objects are never radically different: they are always essences. And the profound leveling or democratizing effect of Santayana's conception of the realm of essence shows itself here, as well. For given that no essence is intrinsically better than any other, there can be no high road to spirituality. The contemplation of God and His attributes, or of the One, is not superior to immediate enjoyment of the color and shape of my big toe. Those who urge the intuition of only selected and approved essences have an agenda beyond spirituality. They are quickly revealed as persons of a practical bent and perhaps zealots, precisely because the spiritual life permits of no agenda and prescribes no preferences.

It is possible, moreover, that spirituality is not an achievement unique to humans. Santayana speculates that a pure or "lyrical" consciousness may well be widespread among animals. Since their minds presumably lack the ability for abstract thought, it is reasonable to assume that the past and the future do not haunt and torture them the way they do us. This should make it significantly easier for them, at least during their inactive hours, to be absorbed in whatever object nature or chance presents. If this is so, the fundamental difference between animals and humans on this point is that what comes naturally to the former, the latter make into an art. Dogs and deer are satisfied with the fortuitous pleasures nature provides; their efforts are confined, when shadows fall, to move back into the sun. Human beings, by contrast, subject themselves to elaborate discipline to enhance and per-

fect their spirituality: we harness the natural by developing the ability
to evoke pure intuitions at will. But it is important to note that all
habits, disciplines, and skills belong to the moral and not to the spiritual life; control over nature or self is gardening, moments of spirituality are the fruit.

Three Stages in the Development of Spirit

The substance-directed stage.   The mind's most frequently experienced condition is bondage to practical interests. This may be
called its substance-directed stage: in it animal faith rivets consciousness upon physical objects. Intuition, though unable to help the psyche
in its struggles, nevertheless mimics its dealings and concerns. The
mind is filled with schemes and purposes: it makes plans for the future,
worries about health and food, and seeks the approval of the neighbors.
The structuring interest of its life is how to do better or at least how
to survive. Accordingly, everything is evaluated from the standpoint
of risk and usefulness, everything is seen as a potential trap or an instrument of prosperity. The groundtone of such a consciousness is set
by fear and rapacity, its preeminent feeling is worry. When things go
well, apprehension is replaced by boisterous frolic or the satiety symbolized by a stupid grin. Much religion is the work of spirit in this
unspiritual phase: the notions of providence, everlasting life, heaven,
and beatitude are inventions of the animal soul in search of security
and unending happiness.

The truth-directed stage.   In studying the movements of matter, we can take an interest in regularities whose scope outstrips our
individual circumstances. When we pursue such general correlations
or causal connections or laws of nature, we tend to pay no heed to the
utility of the particular and focus on the truths it illustrates. In this
truth-directed stage, spirit achieves a level of disinterestedness: its focus is not on private profit or the advancement of animal life, but on
knowledge and understanding for their own sake. Something like this
occurs in science where the practical products of inquiry are incidental
to its goal and conduct. Scientific investigation aims to uncover the
general patterns embodied in the world; this inevitably takes it past
the substance of things to the essence that expresses their relations or
uniform behavior.

Essences thus play a central role in the truth-directed stage of consciousness. Yet even here spirit falls short of spirituality. There are two

reasons for this. First, the search for knowledge, though it may have little immediate application to the needs of the moment, nevertheless constitutes a purposive, worldly enterprise. As such, it involves desire, preference, the restlessness of striving, and the separation of means from end, all of which are signs of the fevered activity of animal life. Second, the forms and formulas that occupy the center of attention in scientific inquiry are not entertained for their own sake. They are taken as truths, not essences; they are prized for what they tell us about existence, not for their splendid self-identity. The truth-directed stage of spirit combines the calm of the realm of truth with continued devotion to the changing patterns of matter.

The essence-directed stage.   Mathematicians sometimes speak of the beauty of their theorems quite independently of whether or not the world happens to embody them. This forgetfulness about existence or sense of its irrelevance keeps the mind within the infinite fields of essence. Since the realm we then explore contains every possible form, there is sufficient variety to provide objects for the contemplation of both mystics and mathematicians. The universals we intuit in this essence-directed stage of consciousness are changeless and reveal nothing about anything beyond themselves. They spread like a painted landscape that is not meant to resemble any place on earth and is yet intrinsically pleasant to behold. The pleasure itself is aesthetic, not physical: it is the exhilaration of thinking and seeing, which is distinct from the belching satisfactions of food and sex. Pure intuition yields delight without engaging the emotions; its object is not romantic feeling but classical form. The musicians of essence, accordingly, are Mozart and Bach, not Puccini or Wagner.

Of course, mathematicians may be dissatisfied with the intuition of established theorems; they will not go far if they cannot get past amazement at the wonderful relation of equality. The drive to discover new relationships or at least to move in an orderly way from essence to essence introduces an element of choice and change into this phase of the growth of mind. To Schopenhauer, who thought that spirituality is a manner of existence, even this small admixture of will was enough to destroy the purity of a holy life. Santayana agrees, of course, that all desire betokens the activity of an animal psyche. But for him this does not render the liberated consciousness psyches sometimes achieve less than spiritual, precisely because he thinks of the spiritual life as fully displayed in each pure intuition. The movement of attention is but an interlude between moments of carefree awareness and takes nothing away from the intrinsic quality of those acts.

Santayana's View of Religion

If religion is the experience and appreciation of eternal things, Santayana's view of the spiritual life is at once his account of religion. He does indeed call the contemplation of essences "ultimate religion"[4] and goes out of his way to show that it is perfectly compatible with his naturalism. But this constitutes only a relatively small part of his discussion of devoutness. On the negative side, he presents a withering critique of theological ideas. And, even though he never formally renounced the Roman Catholicism of his youth, in his personal life he took no interest in the Church either as an institution or as a community.

His view of religious ideas is simple and remained unchanged throughout his long productive life. If they are taken literally, articles of faith are false and constitute bad metaphysics. If we interpret them as symbols, however, they reveal deep moral truths about the human condition. The philosophy of animal faith finds no occasion and has no need to postulate the existence of a God. Following his admired Lucretius, Santayana reminds us that if there were any gods, they would be cosmic accidents, inhabitants of the material world. This, at least, is what they would have to be if they were to have any influence over the course of events; the alternative is a God that is pure spirit and, as such, must remain an impotent observer of developments of nature.

For Santayana, the primary justification for postulating the existence of anything is that we encounter it in the field of action. This immediately presents the theologian with an intolerable dilemma. For if God is conceived as a force in nature, He must be finite and localized, and therefore not the Perfect Being pious people adore. And if God is infinite, He has no foothold in the world, no corner from which to affect or change us; hence we can never have a reason for supposing that He exists. The beings we know cannot be God in the traditional sense; an infinite spirit, by contrast, lacks power and can, therefore, neither act in the world nor be known. We cannot even argue for God's existence in the way we do for other minds. Consciousness is always the actuality or cognitive light of an organism, and there are no psyches exalted enough to warrant the inference that they generate a divine awareness.

Santayana is not content to rest here: he takes the discussion a step beyond the question of the existence of the Deity to the very idea of God. He concludes that the traditional Judeo-Christian concept of God is radically incoherent because it conflates the realms of being and the moral functions any sound philosophy must take special care to distinguish. For God is supposed to be a consciousness that creates the world and guides its destiny. Philosophically, this supposition confounds the realms of spirit and matter; morally, it wrongly mixes generation or origin with the value that results. Even if we thought of the fecundity of matter as divine, we would have to distinguish it from the perfection of knowledge and feeling it creates. There is no principle to hold these ontologically divergent elements together in a single entity. In religious terms, creative power and redeeming love are incompatible: the being characterized by one of these properties cannot display the other, as well.

Natural and Ideal Religion

There are, in fact, two divergent but inadequately distinguished strains within the life of religion that correspond to these irreconcilable theological ideas. Worship can choose as its object either generative power or the fruits of spirit. The former begets a religion of piety toward the source based on a sense of awe at the mystery of becoming and resulting in a submissive or joyous veneration of the creative energy of matter. To call this fertile force "God" is to evince optimism about the prospects of human life in the universe; it is to suppose that the ultimate power is intelligent and caring. Santayana prefers the name "matter" to indicate his conviction that existence is blind, transitory, and not selectively well-disposed toward human beings. If we look at the available evidence abstracted from our hopes, we have to admit that Santayana's tough realism carries the day.

The second tendency within religion is to celebrate the virtues of spirit instead of worshipping the dark machinery of the physical world. There are significant strains in the New Testament (and some in the Old Testament, as well) indicating the turn toward a religion focused on the life of spirit. The account of the passion and resurrection of Jesus Christ, the stress on redemptive love, the willing surrender of divine power implicit in the story of the crucifixion constitute, if read with symbolic reference to the vicissitudes of consciousness, an appreciation in consecrated language of the bondage and deliverance of the human mind. The central issue, Santayana points out in his *The Idea of Christ in the Gospels,* is the identification and liberation of the divine in man, and of this the story of Christ is a permanent and magnificent symbol.

Santayana's view is that only what is of ultimate value should be revered. Power, therefore, is an inappropriate object of worship: the generative order consists of forces and facts that are neither good nor bad. All value depends on the impulses of psyches as these rise to consciousness; the immediate necessary condition of value, therefore, is spirit itself. It is only this world of cognitive light, or selected parts of it, that is properly worthy of celebration. Worship of the generative order—of the Creator or Nature—though understandable in primitive circumstances, serves only to prolong the bondage of spirit. The liberation of consciousness is completed in the ultimate form of religion. In it mind looks away not only from the world of substance but also from the life of spirit to be swallowed up in the eternal. This ultimate religion, as I indicated before, is the spiritual life. It is free of dogma and free of moral constraints; it is religion enjoyed instinctively, without the knowledge of what it is and without religiosity. Only in the spiritual life does the eternal, and thus the ultimate, become immediate.[5]

Reinterpretation of the Nicene Creed

Santayana provides a dramatic display of what he takes to be the confusions in the traditional concept of God in his naturalistic reinterpretation of the Nicene Creed. At the end of the last volume of *Realms of Being,*[6] he notes that God the Father, creator of the world, represents the unfathomable force of matter. This is the power that converts potentiality into actuality, changeless essence into an existential flux. The "assault of reality" on the placid realm of forms is groundless; apart from cheap anthropomorphisms, God's existence and activity are as unintelligible as those of matter. The *mysterium* of religion is thus at once the ultimately incomprehensible existent of a secular ontology.

Since the Nicene Creed takes at this stage the standpoint of the Father, it is not surprising that essence, the Son, is viewed as having been begotten by the primordial force. This means that to the extent that any form *exists,* it derives its status from the movement of matter. But the apparent subordination of essence to matter is counterbalanced by the reminder that everything is created through the Son, which restores form to coeval primacy with force. Santayana's explanation of this idea is that matter without shape and structure would not be anything in particular and hence could neither father nor constitute a cosmos. Generation is possible only by the assumption of form and this makes Father and Son, matter and essence, indispensable partners in the origination of physical things. They are individually necessary and jointly sufficient conditions of the existence of all things.

The third person of the Trinity, the Holy Ghost, obviously represents spirit. Since it "proceeds" from the Father and the Son, it is derivative in its existence. But even though consciousness has it source in the embodiment by matter of complex organic forms, it is nevertheless the giver of life. Here again, life does not mean biological existence but the actuality of cognitive light. Only through spirit do matter and essence come to consciousness of themselves; without it, there would be no spectator or judge of the universe, no love, no feeling, no redeeming intelligence. The Holy Ghost spoke by the prophets; this puts us in mind of spirit's passion for truth and its central role in communication. Just as matter and essence enjoy primacy in their own way, consciousness is first and indispensable in the order of cognition. It is only through its activity that even the Father and Son come to be known.

The remarkable fit between naturalist metaphysics and Christian theology suggests that much of religious thought may well be a symbolic way of conveying truths about the world. Santayana views religion in just this way: he thinks it is a simplified and picturesque articulation of the unconscious wisdom of mankind. Since his own philosophical aim is to develop a sophisticated and conceptually consistent account of the tenets of this common sense or "shrewd orthodoxy," the coincidence of the results should present no surprise.

God and Faith

This philosophical reinterpretation of the Nicene Creed also indicates what Santayana finds wrong with the traditional concept of God. Essence, matter, and spirit are all involved as importantly different factors in the analysis of our experience. The Creed and much subsequent theology unhappily insist on combining them in a single being. This obscures the categoreal differences between them and generates an internally inconsistent notion. No entity can combine changeless synthetic vision with location and function in the flux. And nothing can retain the timelessness of essence once it becomes the cause of physical events. For this reason, God is either eternal essence *or* physical substance *or* feeling consciousness. He cannot be all three, yet being only one is inadequate for divinity.

Santayana's view of religion as a symbolic expression of our deepest insights into the human condition and his persistent comparison of it to poetry, may be thought demeaning to faith. But his intent is neither to offend nor to attack religion. He has the deepest respect, even love, for religious thought and spiritual discipline. His intimate and appreciative knowledge of the sacred books as well as a broad range of theological speculation is repeatedly displayed in his writings. Santayana has no interest in the destruction of religion, only in advancing a proper understanding of its nature. And to say that it is a work of the human imagination is damning only in the eyes of literalists, of people who think that we can have direct knowledge of facts and hence that the creative power of the mind serves only to distort the clear imprints of external reality.

The Symbolism of Religion

As we saw in discussing Santayana's epistemology, he maintains that knowledge is always mediated and symbolic. It is a rendering of the ambient world in terms native to the human mind. All of it involves an element of fancy or free construction; far from impairing the enterprise of cognition, the imagination is actually an indispensable condition of it. Religious thought is not, therefore, in competition with certain, literal, and scientific truth. All symbolism is on the same plane and the cognitive value of religion, as of everything, is a function of what it represents, the adequacy of its symbols to its subject matter, and the improved quality of living it makes possible.

It is only at this point that Santayana's understanding of religion diverges from the popular view. For many think that theology provides an exact description of the real world and that the function of religion is to assure us that the good always prevails, that nothing of value is permanently lost, and that our death and our suffering miraculously open the gates to an endless, better life. Santayana recognizes this view as an expression of animal cravings; the weak, frightened, dying psyche in us wants to be patted on the back and told that the inevitable will not come about. If this is the function of devoutness, it is surely a sham, and religion falls in ill-repute largely because its critics cannot look past the selfish and unspiritual desires that motivate it to the proper role it can play in a full human life.

In Santayana's view, religious thought describes not external reality but the tribulations of the spirit. Its focus is moral in the sense that it deals with consciousness in its struggle to achieve clarity of purpose and self-mastery. All morality in the end is a matter of spirit finding some meaning in its life, for only moments of self-possessed consciousness have intrinsic worth. Accordingly, the function of religion is not to provide animal solace, but to aid in that liberation of the spirit without which the carefree delight of existence can never be savored. The proper aim of religion is not to prepare us for an everlasting existence of animal satisfactions, but to open our eyes to the eternal, to the abundance of the spiritual life possible today.

In this way, the philosophy of animal faith culminates in as rich and sensitive an account of human fulfillment as has ever been conceived. Having begun with skepticism, Santayana gives a persuasive account of knowledge. Being a materialist, he shows a profound appreciation of the conscious, the private, and the eternal. And while insisting on the foundational importance of the animal in us, he provides an understanding of the nature and place of spirituality that is unmatched in soundness and intelligibility. The twentieth century has seen its share of philosophical systems, but none can match Santayana's if boldness of scope, clarity of conception, sanity of judgment, and sensitivity to every aspect of human life are all taken into account.

Chapter Seven

The Enduring Value of Santayana's Philosophy

Some Critics' Views of Santayana

At the end of the previous chapter, I gave Santayana high marks for a well-rounded, intelligible, and sound philosophical system. It is interesting to note that this assessment is not widely shared among professional philosophers. Although *The Life of Reason* had made a significant impact on thought in America, Santayana's later, ontological constructions attracted little following. There are many reasons for this, some of which reveal more about professional philosophy than about the truth or value of his ideas. We must nonetheless consider them if we are to achieve a balanced judgment of Santayana's achievement.

The professionalization of activities in the modern world has established a small group of official philosophers. Not surprisingly, this exclusive community has failed to find Santayana's philosophical work satisfying. They tend to believe that his style is too literary and that his thought lacks technical refinement. He is accused of using outmoded categories, failing to argue for his views, rarely attempting to craft a precise statement of what he means, and substituting an image or a clever phrase where only sustained analysis will do. Many maintain that he is too broad-ranging and interdisciplinary to have been able to make a permanent contribution to any field. Others think that no one as ignorant of the details of science as Santayana professed himself to be, and certainly no one who fails to employ the latest logical tools of philosophy, can produce lasting or interesting work.

Such assessments express testy annoyance rather than damaging objections. In some cases the irritation is with oneself: many a distinguished contemporary philosopher has had an early love affair with Santayana and learned to resist good writing and sweep of thought only with difficulty as a maturing professional. And, in one respect, disregard of Santayana by those for whom philosophy is an occupation is both understandable and appropriate. For his system is more like an essence than a substance: it invites contemplation and enjoyment, not probing dismemberment and piecemeal use. It is not that his ideas lack value even for the professional. But their virtue is their suggestiveness and remarkable scope, not their overt technical sophistication. Consequently, professional philosophers tend to view the system as a dead end leaving them with nothing to do: it is unlikely to found a school in which they could find a place, Santayana's broad and meticulous development of it makes its extension nearly impossible, and it presents no clever moves that could profitably be applied elsewhere. Philosophers today are tinkerers, and Santayana's work is a finished painting.

Santayana as Technical Philosopher

I want to eliminate a possible misunderstanding at once. The fact that Santayana's ontology is not a professional's dream does not mean that it is the work of an ignorant or philosophically unsophisticated mind. Santayana was not only a trained thinker but also a man whose intimate knowledge of the full breadth of philosophical literature is unparalleled in the twentieth century. He read most of the great works of human thought in the language of their origin: Greek and Latin, French and German, English and Spanish were almost equally accessible to him. The library he left contains not only the philosophical classics, but also many of the most significant contemporary works extensively annotated in his hand. He was thoroughly familiar with Heidegger and Whitehead, he wrote stinging critiques of Bergson and Dewey, and he single-handedly convinced Bertrand Russell that the ethical views he shared with G. E. Moore were incorrect. No logically weak intellect could have accomplished this.

A careful reading of Santayana's work reveals, moreover, an unquestioned mastery of the distinctions and conceptual subtleties of philosophy as a specialized discipline. Although Santayana wrote without footnotes, the discerning reader quickly recognizes that he was in continuing dialogue with a wide diversity of philosophical principals. Without explicitly saying so, he anticipated and answered a variety of the most difficult and most sophisticated objections to his ideas. And he showed constant awareness of the conceptual costs of maintaining certain positions; he achieved uncommon consistency by courageously embracing the consequences of his views. Even those who, more modestly, say that Santayana gave no arguments for what he held are wrong. Sustained attention is rewarded with multiple, weighty reasons for each of his contestable ideas, though these considerations are not cast in standard, argumentative form. Such reasonings constitute the concrete and steel structure of his edifice of thought. But his love of architecture taught him early that, important as supports are, they should not have pride of place in the fine rooms of the house.

To those who object that Santayana's categories are old-fashioned we can respond with the reminder that even in cars, where the model changes every year, the latest is not always the best. Philosophy, in particular, need not be infatuated with the new. There is no reason to believe that current drama is better than Shakespeare, or that Quine, Carnap, and a collection of recent articles makes Plato obsolete. Such notions as substance and matter and truth do, indeed, have a history, but that past should not count against them when they are put to contemporary use. And that is precisely what Santayana did and did better than anyone else in the last hundred years. He adapted the great, traditional concepts of philosophy to articulate a thoroughly modern view. In it, scholastic categories are stripped to fighting weight: form, as we saw, retains its meaning as nature or structure but loses teleology, spirit remains the inmost part of man but is set free from everything occult and from theology. Such concepts should be assessed individually, on the basis of the work they do. We must not suppose them worthless because they are old; their virtue is to connect modern insights with traditional thoughts.

The Task of Philosophy

That Santayana's style is literary, even poetic, is clearly true. That it is too literary is a condemnation based on an idea of what philosophy should be. Such ideas are typically controversial and ill-supported: they belong to the ultimate presuppositions of a system of thought rather than among its substantiated results. When someone says, therefore, that a person with whom he disagrees on a set of identifiable conceptual topics is not really doing philosophy, we must interpret his comments as an exercise in rhetoric. We all want to reach for the high ground, which it is easiest to do by denying the legitimacy of our opponent's enterprise.

Rhetoric apart, however, there is a real disagreement here between

Santayana and his critics. Some philosophers think their task is similar to and dependent on science: they are to take the results of the scientific endeavor and, by investigation and reasoning closely akin to it, develop theories of the greatest generality. Others urge us to abandon all hope for their ancient discipline: everything of importance will be discovered by science, is already embodied in ordinary speech, or has long been revealed by the deity. Those who favor the former view want to make philosophy into a precise and technical subject, while those committed to the latter busy themselves with exploding the grand illusions of the generalizers.

Santayana disagreed with both groups. We have noted before that he thought all of language and all knowledge constitute but a tenuous, symbolic grasp of the real. Science discloses, therefore, neither the literal nor the absolute truth about the world. Familiarity with it is useful and important, but we must not suppose that it resolves all the problems of human life and of philosophy. We have also much to learn from philosophical reflection on science, common sense, religion, and the most general features of reality. Even if, as Santayana clearly believed, the common sense of mankind embodies in its practices the soundest philosophy, there is need for discerning thought to raise the tenets of this animal faith to explicit consciousness, to clarify them, to distinguish them from the arbitrary dogmas that overlay them in the public mind, and to shape them into a consistent whole. Since the task of philosophy is to stimulate reflective thought, its content must be discursively defensible but its language must be evocative and rich. In this way, it can summon up those essences of great generality whose contemplation helps to make sense of our life experience.

This view of the contribution of philosophy appears to me to be thoroughly sensible. It avoids the absurd pretension of claiming preeminence for the field and certainty for its results. But it clearly affirms that though philosophy is not the queen of the sciences, neither is it the meaningless ravings of deluded minds. Philosophical thought plays a central role in the modest enterprise of human knowledge. It is of course, as all thought, optional. But once we embark on the enterprise of trying to understand life instead of merely living it, sound reflection on the irreducibly different features of existence, on human nature, and on the good life becomes essential. Philosophers can then employ their critical skills, their ability to see connections, and their imagination to devise theories about the nature of the world and about the proper place of human beings in it. Their products will lack certain truth—everything does—but they will, in varying measures, enhance our understanding of ourselves.

Naturalistic Approach to Language

There is another issue connected with language and philosophy that should be mentioned here. For many centuries, philosophy was concerned with human beings and the realities that surround them. This direct interest in persons and objects was largely replaced, in the early years of the modern world, by overwhelming worries about our cognitive apparatus. The preoccupation with thought itself yielded to primary concern with language during the present century. The belief seems to have gained currency among some philosophers that since language mediates our cognitive contact with the world, the best or the only way to discern the general features of reality is by attending to the way we articulate or shape them through our speech.

It is to Santayana's great credit that he did not fall prey to either of these unfortunate tendencies. It is not, of course, that he failed to take an interest in thought and language. But his approach to them was that of a naturalist and not of someone who thinks that they are unconditioned, foundational realities. He saw them, in other words, in their organic, historical, and social context as human responses to a baffling and threatening world. He used them with an understanding of their potential and with care not to exceed their limits. He was, above all, skeptical of any panacea, any single factor that explains or determines everything, and any human activity claimed to be world creative. Paradoxically perhaps, because he thought nearly as well as can be thought, he did not overestimate the power of reflection, and his superb command of language saved him from being overly impressed by what it can do.

The Beauty of Santayana's Thought

What, then, is the current significance and lasting value of Santayana's philosophy? Nearly all who know it would concede that it is an exquisite system of thought. The simple beauty of the conception is matched by the elegance of the writing that conveys it. The reader comes away with the satisfaction of having felt her mind soar and her soul uplifted. The very thinking of such thoughts is a source of joy:

the clarity of its ideas, the interconnection of its parts, the bold sweep of its conclusions all conspire to make the system a worthy object of contemplation on its own account.

This is the sort of compliment one is inclined to pay Spinoza and the other masters of beautiful thought. And it would, indeed, constitute the highest commendation if philosophy were a purely artistic endeavor in search of ideas that are aesthetically pleasing or sublime. But the ideal of philosophy is more difficult and more complex than that: in order to achieve it, we must seek ideas that are, in accord with the classical dictum, not only beautiful but also good and true, without the platonic assurance that whichever have one of these features must have the others, as well.

Do His Ideas Advance the Human Good?

I interpret the question of whether or not Santayana's ideas are good as asking about their value for the purposes of life. We must not take usefulness in too narrow a sense here: philosophical ideas are not meant to help us make better refrigerators or sell more cars. Their job is to advance understanding and appreciation, to guide us in leading the good life, and to help us organize society along just and rational principles. It is impossible, of course, for the judgments we make about such things to be objective or certain, for the issues of what is good and just and rational, of what constitutes understanding, and of what we should appreciate are themselves open to philosophical debate. But we should, nevertheless, be able to make some assessments that will command the assent of people of goodwill and sound common sense.

Santayana belongs in the naturalistic tradition of Lucretius and Hobbes. He viewed human beings as having their home in the world, as continuous with the animals and material objects which constitute a single, vast cosmos. If there is transcendence of our animal status, it is not physical: we do not live beyond the time our bodies wear out and never get relocated to a safer clime. What happens to us here, moreover, is fraught with danger, and the sure solution to any of our problems constantly eludes us. A search for the meaning of life beyond the parameters of earthly existence is, therefore, pointless. And the dream of certainty in cognitive and moral matters leads only to intolerance in blind dogmatists and disappointment among the discerning.

This naturalization of the human and concurrent rejection of the search for certainty hit exactly the right note for the advancement of

our good. Even if there is a God and a life or significance in the hereafter, given our woeful and necessary ignorance it is best for us to think
that this is all. We can then concentrate our efforts on achieving full
potential in this life by making our days rich with everything worthwhile humans can do and enjoy. In case this sounds self-seeking or
hedonistic, let us remember that Santayana took anything but a narrow
view of our perfection. His sensitivity to friendship, religious feeling,
and the arts suggests that we should think of fulfillment as involving,
at least potentially for each of us, the highest, most spiritual, and most
generous activities of the race. It is just that, contrary to what his
teacher William James had thought, Santayana was convinced that we
do not need to believe in a supernatural destiny in order to lead the
best life and to attain full achievement. If we were cynical, we could
say that it is best to act throughout life as though we were marked for
extinction and then, mindful of uncertainty or in the way of insurance,
at the end confess our sins and register a quick apology.

The Centrality of Individuals

Santayana espoused, once again, the most useful view in maintaining the central significance of individuals. He thought that the psyche
is the source of the preferences which ground morality and that consciousness comes, at least in humans, in personal form. As subjects of
feeling and centers of action, individuals constitute the ultimate units
of the moral world. This position places Santayana at the opposite pole
from Hegel and those others who aver that persons are but fragments
of larger, organic wholes (such as the state) against which they have no
legitimate claim and within which alone they may hope to attain fulfillment. Such views are scandalous in their blatant subordination of
the person to supposedly higher, but in fact derivative and insentient,
beings. There is really no such thing as society or the state apart from
individuals and their intricate interactions. And it is pernicious to believe that there is, for such conviction leads to the restriction of liberty,
to abandoning responsibility for oneself, and to treating persons as
though they did not matter. Santayana was in close agreement with
the existentialists on this point; the shared view, when embraced, issues in self-determination with respect to both cognitive and moral
matters. Adopting it makes it more likely that we take charge of our
lives, choose what to believe, how to live and what to do, and bear
without complaint the consequences of our decisions.

Relativism and Toleration

An additional result of the high value placed on individuals is respect for others. This respect is reinforced by another of Santayana's moral ideas. The relativity of values he championed leads, as we saw, to toleration of the divergent commitments and projects of our fellows. There may be no thought more important to embrace than this sound relativism: if we believed that the differing lifestyles, moral values, religious beliefs, and political ideas of others were no less legitimate than ours, if we could even just view them as matters of indifference to us, the world would be a strikingly better place. Santayana provided the philosophical underpinnings for this humane acceptance of our diversity, but the world has not been quick to adopt his belief. Freedom to display our nature, intelligent responsibility in actualizing it, and unflinching devotion to staying out of other people's business—autonomy and toleration, in other words—could raise human life from the level of stupid struggle to lasting happiness.

I do not want to depict Santayana as a visionary or a reformer. In his early work he saw some hope for mankind and found evidences of development—as a subtitle to *The Life of Reason* he chose *The Phases of Human Progress*—but even there he avoided a prescriptive tone. His later writing reveals that his attitude was that of an observer who merely notes facts and possibilities. He did not think that urging people to adopt certain views or to act in novel ways was very useful; if they were kindred souls, spontaneous sympathy would point them in his direction. His conviction was that both the beliefs which move us and what we do are expressions of our individual natures, and these constitutions are not easily changed. In spite of his unwillingness to advocate his ideas, however, it is appropriate for us to assess their utility and to reflect on what effects they would have if they were generally adopted.

The Choice of Self

This mention of individual natures leads me to a point of significant weakness in Santayana's thought. His relativism opens the door to the appreciation of every possible nature, but gives us no guidance in choosing one for our own. It is tempting to say that biological and social conditions render the psyche fully determinate and leave only the need for self-knowledge and self-actualization. But Santayana himself stressed that the world is full of contingency and open ends: we choose our natures as much as we find them. One of the great traditional tasks of moral philosophy has been to indicate the sorts of character traits and lifestyles it is appropriate to have. To be sure, relativism must surrender all claim to universality in these matters. But it need not give up the educative task of framing guidelines or general principles by reference to which we can make hopefully satisfying choices.

Yet Santayana showed little interest in helping us with these personal decisions. The closest he came to a useful principle was in his discussion of the life of reason. But even there, he suggested only that we might strive for the largest possible number of compatible satisfactions and said nothing substantive about what desires to foster and which pleasures to embrace. Aristotle, whom Santayana admired, had had no hesitation in giving a detailed account of the virtues, with suitable flexibility to accommodate individual differences. Nevertheless, Santayana failed to follow his example and thus abandoned one of the vital missions of philosophy.

His unwillingness to advise us concerning the choices that shape our nature was extended by Santayana to a general reluctance to indicate what sorts of psyches we might foster in our children and what manner of persons our society might be wise to create. Appreciation of diversity appears to have left him without a principle of choice, and distressingly, we find that the magnificent scope of his system does not include a significant contribution to the philosophy of education. Even his social and political thought suffers from the same unwillingness to give guidance to human endeavor as affects his morality. It is not that he himself lacked preferences concerning the structuring values and political institutions of society. And it is certainly not that sensible people lack sympathy with his refusal to anoint his own choices and pronounce them universal values. But if we read philosophy so we may lead better lives, it does not help much to be told that each individual must be true to his or her nature and every community must live by its deepest values. Self-realization as an ethical view goes well with universal determinism. But if we leave any room for choice, the neat simplicity of following what nature imposes evaporates and we feel directionless and baffled in our freedom.

I am not currently interested in whether or not Santayana's relativistic self-actualization view of morality is in some sense true. My task now is to explore the value of his ideas, that is, their likely consequences if they were embraced. And there I find that, salutary as his toleration would prove, the moral system that decrees it is deficient in giving us guidance for life. Santayana may well respond by reminding us that the primary task of philosophy is to understand; once that is accomplished, sensible action naturally follows. We, in turn, can agree with him on the importance of intellectual grasp and even on the correctness of the classical claim that to understand is at once to forgive all. The problem is precisely that, in Santayana's case, no actions and no principles of action seem to flow from the intelligence that lays hold of the nature of things. This is why he has been said to be primarily contemplative in his interests. The charge is not without some justice, but the source of its rightness is not that Santayana himself had little sympathy for the life of action. It is rather that here, as elsewhere in his thought, appreciation of how things are crowds out any desire to change them.

Celebration of the Present

This aesthetic and contemplative attitude is reinforced by the clear identification and acknowledged omnipresence of essences. Consciousness of the present form of things enables us to detach them, at least in thought, from their history, context, and consequences. The resulting immediacy, as we saw in earlier discussions of the skeptical reduction and of the spiritual life, is without ulterior meaning or use. But precisely because it appears unconnected to anything else, it can be enjoyed without reservation and for its own sake alone. This discovery is by no means unique to Santayana: even Aristotle spoke of the sort of activity in which means and end collapse and we take spontaneous pleasure in what we see or do, and Santayana himself credited Proust with discerning the bittersweet beauty of essences in his wonderful reflections on past experience. But no one before Santayana had made the realm of essence the centerpiece of his thought and no one before him had succeeded in developing the systematic ontological foundations of wholesale appreciation.

The insight that we can celebrate the present is of particular significance in a society devoted to results and to the future. Our urge for improving our condition and for eventual outcomes sets us at risk of losing the only sure satisfaction available to us. The impatient pursuit of what is yet to be tends to blind us to the formed magnificence of everything that surrounds us. This restlessness results in dissatisfaction with everything—although we cannot stop competing in the rat race, we know it is not one we can ever win. Santayana's reminders that the world is here to enjoy, that anxiety can be lifted by attention to the immediate, that the form of anything is intrinsically delightful to behold are potent antidotes to the tumult and haste of our ways. A measure of indifference to the future and firm concentration on what is at hand yield internal peace. They help us recapture the playfulness and beauty, the very soul we lost.

The clear definition of the realm of essence has the additional value of showing the continuity of literature and the fine arts with mathematics, the works of private imagination, and logic. All of them are explorations of the infinite reaches of essence by the human mind in its disciplined or playful moments. The essences and their relations may differ from case to case, but it is a major step toward enhanced understanding to realize that, throughout them all, we deal only with qualities and relations, that is, with forms. If we keep this in mind, it becomes much easier to appreciate the contemporary arts. For the shapes of existing things reproduced on canvas, for example, are not preferable as forms to unfamiliar, abstract color patches. In presenting us with nonrepresentational shapes, the artist may want to draw our attention away from the physical things that evoke a penumbra of emotions and ideas of ulterior use. Only in this way, she might think, can she focus our minds on the intrinsic qualities of the painting alone. Once practical interest in physical objects is removed, we can begin to take truly aesthetic delight in the pure forms of color, shape, structure, rhythm, and sound. Ideas such as these, which help us understand and enjoy otherwise unappreciated portions of our experience, are not without social usefulness and personal value.

A Comprehensive Scheme of Concepts

There is a final issue about what good Santayana's philosophy might be or do that I want briefly to mention. Many of us seek an understanding in cosmic terms of our place in the world. Religions and ideologies have always gained adherents through their ability to give a simple and clear general account of human nature and prospects. It is unfortunate that, for the most part, philosophers have abandoned the effort to develop such comprehensive conceptual schemes. For, in this field, it is primarily to them that we must look for novel ideas of scope and critical sophistication. Dispassionate reason is unlikely to rein in those looking for converts or political supporters.

I began my discussion of the value of Santayana's philosophy with comments about the virtues of his naturalism. I now want to add the less controversial point that, even if there is disagreement about the details or orientation of his metaphysics, the fact that he presented a fully articulated system is significant. For such an edifice of ideas encourages people to think boldly, yet carefully, about the great problems of human existence. And reflection that is imaginative, systematic, and critical might enable us to come to terms with, perhaps even to gain intellectual dominion over, our fate.

Not only does Santayana's systematic thought stimulate reflection, it may itself be wholly or partly acceptable to a number of intelligent people. In a world in which ultimate questions cannot be resolved with certainty, there is some advantage to be gained simply from having a variety of plausible alternatives readily available. So long as choice in such matters is not foreclosed by religious or political oppression, Santayana's vision will always exert a powerful attraction over urbane minds. Those who remain dissatisfied have everyone's best wishes in their quest to "clean better," as Santayana says, "the windows of their soul," even if their success at that task is quite improbable.

Are Santayana's Ideas True?

In assessing the probable truth of Santayana's ideas, we face an immediate technical problem. Truth, for him, is the indelible record of essences exemplified in the world. All truth relates, therefore, to the flux of matter and to the minds it generates. But Santayana's ontology ranges beyond the existent to the realm of essence. To say that his thoughts are true would thus be to maintain, among other things, that the infinity of the realm of forms is somehow instantiated in finite material substance. This is not only impossible, it also subverts the very distinction he drew between existent matter and intrinsically nonexistent forms.

This is no doubt a part of the reason why Santayana thought of philosophy as the evocation of essences of a very high level of generality, rather than as the description of substance. I have indicated before that its function is to develop a set of ideas in terms of which we can helpfully think about the world and our place in it. Some of these notions, such as that the values we hold are grounded in our preferences, can be true and Santayana must claim that they are; others, such as that there is an infinite number of essences, cannot be true in the sense to which Santayana limits the term. I do not think that this technical restriction of the notion of truth is of any great significance; I will, accordingly, interpret the question of the truth of his philosophy as one asking about its correctness or conceptual defensibility.

Santayana and Positivism

Let me warn at once that neither truth nor correctness is, for Santayana, a matter of verification. Logical empiricists have made much of the supposed need of propositions to be testable by sense experience in order to have any meaning. But they have not been able to render their own principle of verification meaningful in terms of the criterion it enunciates and, in any case, they have far too restrictive a view of human experience. It is not that Santayana is without the positivist tendencies of which logical empiricism was a natural outcome. He maintained, for example, an inflexible distinction between facts and values, and surrendered to science final authority in the knowledge of nature. But while such commitments clearly separate him from phenomenologists, they do not set the groundtone of his philosophy. And he specifically eschewed the narrow empiricism and the antimetaphysical excesses of the positivists of his day. One could well say that he adopted only the sensible tough-mindedness of positivism without falling victim to its sweeping, self-destructive dogmas.

Most of those who object to the realm of essence do so on account of rigid commitment to a parsimonious, empiricist view of reality. Occam's razor admonishes us never to postulate entities unnecessarily; this is taken by some thinkers as the warrant for rejecting whatever is not an object of science or ordinary belief. Now, admittedly, the notion of an infinity of forms appears to go against our normal intuitions. But this is largely because unreflective common sense lacks conceptual sophistication and people tend, in any case, to be inattentive to their ontology.

Reality and Power

Our practical orientation makes us suppose that anything real must in relevant respects resemble the physical objects with which we deal every day. This general conviction was converted into hallowed dogma by Plato when he identified reality with the possession of power. Even those who say, more cautiously, that in the last analysis every difference must make a difference, rely on this dubious and unsupported principle. Santayana is among the very few philosophers in the history of Western thought who recognized its arbitrariness, and he may well be the only major one who framed his system in specific defiance of it. The reason people object to his powerless, eternal essences is not because he is incorrect in distinguishing them from other sorts of beings, but because they misunderstand the nature of this type of reality.

In fact, essences easily meet Occam's rigorous demand. To the attentive person, their recognition is as inescapable as the admission of the existence of water and umbrellas on a rainy day. The difference is in the sort of being we claim to have identified and the evidence for our finding. Since essences are not physical things, we do not encounter them in our actions. They are not full-bodied objects whose potentialities hold threat or promise and whose existence is a matter of belief. Their being is that of temporally indeterminate qualities and relations considered in isolation from the context in which we find them in the world. Each is simply and timelessly itself, a specific reality ready to be conceived or to be adopted to give form to some existence.

Are Essences Properties of Objects Only?

We might say that essences are minimal realities in that, although they may become the properties of objects, they themselves have no properties. Accordingly, to speak of them in propositional terms is to distort their nature somewhat: our proper approach to them is through the inwardness of pure intuition. This should make it clear that, though their recognition has profound philosophical consequences, we do not commit ourselves to anything controversial about the furniture of the universe by embracing the claim that essences are real. For Santayana was emphatic in denying that essences exist; they are, he claimed, merely the forms of definiteness without which nothing could gain a foothold in the flux.

Someone might object here that all this means simply is that essences are the results of abstraction. Their role is to serve as the qualities of things or as the relations which connect them; when we wrench them out of context they may appear to have independent being, but they are in reality only aspects or features of natural objects. This argument would carry some weight were it not for two obvious replies Santayana can make. First, it is easy to focus on essences which are not and will perhaps never be embodied in the physical world. And there

are some forms, such as that of the square circle, the good, and the
Deity, which can in the nature of the case never come to characterize
anything in the flux. If this is so, essences must have some status other
than that proper to the features of material things.

The second reply takes us back to the centrality, for Santayana's
philosophy, of the skeptical reduction and of the spiritual life. For, in
both, we encounter essences in their purity, unattached to anything
existent. There is nothing abstract about such experiences, or else we
would have to say that the piccolo is abstract when it plays without
the rest of the band. To be sure, the essences present in pure intuition
can become components of richer wholes. But that does not imply that
they must be understood as intrinsically belonging there or having no
independent status. To argue for these latter claims, the critic needs
the principle of the ontological primacy of physical objects, and it is
extremely difficult to make that proposition more than an ungrounded
dogma. I conclude that, the disagreement of a large part of the philosophical establishment notwithstanding, Santayana was probably correct in assigning a special, separate ontological status to essences.

Matter as an Ontological Category

Santayana's conception of matter fails to share the success of his view
of essences. He was certainly right in not adopting any particular conception of the nature of matter; philosophy should leave such issues for
exploration by the sciences. But looking to science for the empirical
details does not absolve Santayana of the need to give an account of
matter as an ontological category. If we take the role matter plays in
his system seriously, however, it is intrinsically impossible to meet this
requirement. For, as I indicated before, the force of matter is simply
that factor which, without intelligence and purpose, selects certain
essences for embodiment and summons them into existence. If we look
for the feature of matter that makes this remarkable feat possible, we
are sure to be disappointed. Each characteristic is an essence, and essences, being impotent, are unable to accomplish their own actualization. As a result, there can be nothing specific in matter that is
responsible for existence. And, since matter is simply that which renders essences existent, it can itself have no nature, not even the nature
of giving embodiment to forms.

From time to time, Santayana saw this consequence clearly and thought that it was equivalent to saying that matter is a groundless force and that existence is a surd. At other times, however, he did not hesitate to give elaborate descriptions of what he said was the realm of matter. In fact, of course, these accounts were not of matter as an ontological category but of what we might call the material world or, in his language, substance. It is perfectly appropriate to discuss the nature of substance because it is a compound of matter and form; but such disquisitions do not in the least advance our understanding of the material, that is, the faceless and natureless, component of existing things. The reason they do not help is that, if matter has no essence, intellectual grasp of it is impossible. Even symbolic knowledge is beyond the pale: the use of any essence to shed light on the formless is both hopeless and radically misleading.

Existence a Surd

We may well sympathize with Santayana in his conviction that the world, existence itself, is at bottom an unintelligible surd. But since the work of thought is to increase our understanding, it is not easy to incorporate such a belief into one's philosophy. It might be possible as a conclusion of sustained inquiry. But it is suspect if built into a fundamental category of the system. The greatest problem, of course, is that a concept of what is truly unintelligible can itself not be understood. The notion of a breakdown of reason, as we find it in a contradiction, is easily grasped. The idea of the formless, however, is a thought of something without content, hence the thought not even of a something, an empty thought. It is odd that we seem, nevertheless, to have some inkling of what Santayana had in mind. But it is dubious that whatever this subjective feeling comes to is adequate for purposes of philosophy.

The difficulties Santayana had with the conceptualization of matter may appear minor when measured against the truths his position suggests. If we think of matter as an arational force restlessly actualizing set after set of essences, it is natural to view the world as perpetually changing. All the processes of material substance will then appear as finite and contingent, and we will have to embrace the idea that nothing *must* exist and probably nothing will endure. Our expectation of uniformity in the physical world is just that: nature's hands are not tied by its past. It is also not bound by devotion to a law or the love of some worthy result. No master plan is being actualized in what takes place and, if there is development in some particulars, it may last awhile or else may be soon reversed.

All of this appears to be just right. By saying so I do not mean to imply that it is uncontroversial or that it can be established conclusively. If anything, the preponderance of philosophers in the history of thought have rejected these ideas. But the advance of science and the secularization of the modern world have made them attractive to a growing number of people, and they now constitute the indispensable core of what perhaps the majority of intellectuals maintain. A natural corollary of these views is the belief that indubitable knowledge of existence is impossible and hence the very quest for certainty is ill-conceived and inappropriate. Here again, Santayana appears to be right on the mark, championing an idea that is in line with current intuitions and which in the long run is likely to prevail. His rejection of wholesale skepticism as a view incompatible with the beliefs on which we happily act did not leave him altogether gullible or insensitive to the limits of the human frame.

Is Truth Reducible to Essence and Matter?

Santayana claimed that each of his four realms constitutes an irreducibly different mode of being. This is easily seen concerning essence, matter, and spirit, but seems not to be correct about truth. He himself said repeatedly that the entire realm of truth is but a portion of the realm of essence, namely the segment selected by matter for actualization. This means that truth is, in fact, reducible to matter and essence and represents the area of their intersection. Santayana may well have been more accurate, therefore, if he spoke only of three realms and used truth as a neat example to demonstrate the explanatory power of his categories.

However this may be, the conception of truth as an objective standard against which our opinions must be gauged is a welcome and appropriate corrective to the current wave of historicism. That context, perspective, language, conceptual framework, and purpose have a profound bearing on how we see things is beyond dispute. But this does not imply the absence of an objective reality that is altogether independent of human purposes and cognitive activity. Whatever we think of the matter or however we view it, either there are English-speaking owls on Mars or there are not. And however we feel about it, Lenin either suffered from syphilis or he did not, and the difficulty of ascertaining which was the case and the elaborate explanations of why we cannot know do nothing to change the hard facts. It is to the celebration of such unalterable realities that Santayana's ideas about truth are dedicated.

A Problem with His Notion of Truth

But, even though Santayana's heart is in the right place, there is a problem with his conception of truth. Let us suppose that an owl hoots near my house one night. That it did is a fact or a truth about the world. Suppose further that I hear the sound and think it is the horn of the taxi I called. It is also true that, to someone with my expectations who occupies a point in space distant from the bird, the hoot sounds like a horn. Santayana calls such apprehensions (or misapprehensions) of a truth its "radiations." The radiations of any given truth spread in all directions and include every relation in which it stands to things, essences, and minds. While this sounds innocuous and perhaps even right, it has the unfortunate consequence of replacing every error with a truth. For the view commits us to maintaining that whatever is perceived or conceived by us in however bizarre a way, is just so for us and represents a cognitive achievement. We can, of course, change our opinion of the matter, but that is only to trade truth for truth. What makes one of these truths preferable to the others? Surely not that one is *more true,* because truth has no degrees and thus every true perception and each true judgment is perfectly and fully true. What authority does the original truth we misperceive hold? None as truth, for every distorted appearance of it shares the dignity of its status. Remarkably, then, we cannot escape being always right, and this robs truth of its normative function as the standard we aim to attain.

Can Santayana offer an adequate solution to this problem? I think he can, but not within the limits of his theory of truth. He must explain why, for example, only the truth that it was an owl that hooted is an appropriate stopping place for the inquiring mind and hearing it as a taxi's horn must be rejected as a misperception. The insistence that we must seek to find how things are and not how they appear may well be right, but there is no basis for it if, as Santayana maintains, realities and their appearances share equal truth. Fact and its misperceptions, however, have differential value for purposes of action. Taking an owl's hoot for a taxi's horn will not get me to town quicker, and if I keep taking the taxi's horn to be an owl, the cab will leave. We may well suppose, therefore, that the authority of the objective truth derives from its ability to guide intelligent action. Santayana could maintain that it is this consideration, extraneous to the status of any embodied essence as a truth, that compels us to pay special heed to perspective-independent facts, to that part of the realm of truth constituted by how things are and not how they appear. Although he barely hinted at this view, it is clearly in line with his repeated insistence on the importance of action. It also shows his close relationship to pragmatism without, however, implying that he actually adopted the pragmatic theory of truth.

Science and Ordinary Experience

Every modern philosopher since Descartes has been confronted with the need to reconcile the world view of science with the facts of direct experience. Physics, the most advanced of the sciences, offers us a picture of nature as a spatially extended continuum of matter and energy. Each event in this world-process can presumably be explained by reference to physical entities alone, along with the laws that govern their operation. This means that science has no need of, and leaves no room for, the feelings, moods, purposes, perspectives, and mistakes that are the staple of private experience. The stationary desk that I perceive as solid and smooth is, for science, a jagged collection of whirling atoms separated by empty space. The brilliant sunset that fills my soul with joy is but an astronomical and atmospheric configuration resulting in a stream of photons striking the retina; my joy itself is simply the electrical activity of cells in the brain. Although we use the same word to denote them, even the space of physics and the space of ordinary experience are different: the former is a centerless, boundless continuum, while the latter is centered on the body and is limited by the changing horizon. Physical time is uniform and regular; the time of subjective experience pulsates, speeding up and slowing down in accordance with our moods. The recurrent and pressing problem that has occupied philosophers for hundreds of years is how these apparently incompatible conceptual structures are related to each other or how both can be accommodated in a philosophical system.

Reductive materialists have generally supposed that the scientific view is true and experience is understandable illusion. Phenomenologists, by contrast, have taken direct experience as fundamental and limited the truth of the scientific world picture to that of a useful abstraction. Comprehensive thinkers have attempted to give each conceptual framework its due, but only at the expense of bizarre dialectical principles or verbal sleights of hand. Santayana's major philosophical achievement may well lie in the remarkable way in which he managed to do justice to both science and experience without invoking a specious dialectic. The scientific enterprise, he held, gives or will at some point in the future give an adequate account of the material world. But this leaves religion, art, and subjective experience paramount in their own sphere: they are the highlights in the life of mind.

The Philosophy of Mind at the Center

How can the two different enterprises and their divergent conceptual results be reconciled? By having as their objects distinct realms of being. Science focuses on physical reality and phenomenology on consciousness: separate but equally real subject matter assures diverse methods and results, along with shared legitimacy. How are the two realms that serve as differentiating objects related? They are ontologically irreducible, even though, from the standpoint of origins, matter grounds the existence of consciousness. This makes it clear that Santayana's philosophy of mind is at the very center not only of his account of the nature of man, but also of his attempt to accommodate both the austere findings of science and the enriching dimensions of personal and social experience in a single, sensible system of thought. Epiphenomenalism is the price he had to pay for retaining both of these important elements of human life and for assuring autonomy to each.

Admittedly, the view that mind is an impotent by-product of organic processes sounds odd and appears to conflict with our everyday intuitions. We seem, after all, to experience consciousness as a participant in intelligent actions and we believe that, in the form of will, it is a direct cause of a variety of effects. Yet if science can account for the occurrence of every event, there is neither need nor room for the causal efficacy of private consciousness. The impotent mind hypothesis is, therefore, the penultimate stage in developing the implications of the adequacy of science in the explanation of the world-process. The final conclusion, which Santayana vigorously resisted, is that consciousness as a subjective phenomenon does not exist at all. To be able to evaluate epiphenomenalism, it must be seen in this context: it is a compromise position designed to salvage what is viable in mind-body dualism and to avoid the absurdities of the reductive materialist.

Those who maintain the impotence of mind do so not because their view recommends itself as the most plausible on first analysis. They tend to adopt it as the position that is the least costly and least improbable once all the facts are taken into account. For of the classic mind-body theories, interactionist dualism is incompatible with well-established facts of science, and the unconnected parallel development of consciousness and the physical world strains all credulity. Moreover, the counter-intuitiveness of epiphenomenalism pales beside the materialist's audacity in supposing all of the colored life of mind to be a stinging illusion.

Is Mind Impotent?

None of this means, of course, that the impotence hypothesis is without its budget of difficulties. Its initial implausibility, its apparent conflict with some of our most firmly held beliefs, and our palpable experience of the involvement of consciousness in such activities as reasoning all bear against the view. The greatest difficulty resides in providing a theoretically adequate account of how physical events can give rise to ontologically unconnected and causally inert moments of consciousness. The difference between the substantial processes of nature and thin, transcendental, synthetic intuitions is so momentous that Santayana's repeated comment about the unintelligibility of all generation leaves us, particularly in this case, baffled and dissatisfied. His attempts to relate matter and mind in terms of the connection between Aristotle's notions of potentiality and second act remained undeveloped hints, and as an old man he felt obliged to remark that on this point he had "not seen much new light."[1]

Our view of the success of much of Santayana's system depends on our evaluation of epiphenomenalism. Yet precisely because the theory is so central and because the issues are so complex and so broad, it is impossible to pass a judgment that could command even majority assent. Here arguments do not appear compelling, and personal taste and philosophical predisposition come to the fore. I shall leave the matter with my own reasoned assessment. So long as the mind-body problem is cast in the traditional terms developed by Descartes, epiphenomenalism is the least inadequate solution. A reconceptualization of this entire field would be welcome and perhaps not impossible to achieve. But, short of that, both the weight of the evidence and the theory's compatibility with a rich collection of established views and human activities favor the impotence hypothesis.

His Individual Relativism

Ethicists are, for the most part, an intolerant lot: many of them feel that no action which fails to conform to universal rules can belong in the sphere of morality. Such insistence on uniformity concerning what is right or good tends to be based on intuitions acquired in a liberal society and is reinforced by the silent thought that universal morality is the last and highest stage of human development. The more abstractly we formulate this principle, the more irresistibly right it will seem; its groundlessness cannot be seen so long as we suppose that morality is unrelated to the predicaments of human life.

Aristotle and others who recognized the organic connection between who we are and what we value would have been relativists in ethics had they not been committed, for independent and altogether inadequate reasons, to a universal, fixed, and normative human nature. If we take the testimony of history seriously and reject this fictive identity of the human essence, the temptation to think of ethics in absolute and in pandemic terms evaporates.

In spite of the shrillest chorus of professional moralists, therefore, Santayana was surely right in insisting on the relative and context-bound nature of all value judgments. We may indeed feel that some actions are more and others less humane, that the good some embrace is rigid and impoverishing while our own is inclusive and generous. But all such thoughts, feelings, intuitions, and judgments presuppose a standard, tacit perhaps but firmly held, by which we measure what we see and what befalls us. These standards can, of course, themselves be evaluated, although not without reference to yet other, possibly broader or more satisfying, criteria. Both values and valuations are, therefore, conditional: they depend on our commitments and preferences which, in turn, are products of the individual nature heredity, social circumstances, chance events, and personal choices create for each of us.

Santayana is right, moreover, that much, though not all, of absolutistic morality amounts to the demand that others be like us and to their satisfying condemnation when they are not. From this standpoint, to adopt relativism is to outgrow the childishness of parents, which is the comfort of supposing that we know the right course for everyone. It is worth stressing that on this view values are relative not to how we feel or what we think, but to our individual nature embodied in the structure and dispositions of the psyche. There is a great deal, of course, that human psyches share; these similarities make social life possible and are, in turn, fostered by it. The important point is, however, that the differences are not negligible and they are reflected in permanent and sometimes irreconcilable divergences in our commitments.

Spirituality for All?

Had Santayana recommended spirituality and the detachment it involves as a form of life, and the highest form, at that, he would have been both wrong and inconsistent. The impartial readiness to welcome whatever comes along is an ideal for consciousness alone and presupposes continued severe selectivity on the physical level of the psyche's operations. And given his commitment to the relativity of values, no pattern of actions and satisfactions can constitute *the* best life, only the best for persons of a certain nature. In fact, of course, Santayana was careful not to make either of these claims: he thought that pure intuitions are momentary fruitions of organic process and can be called a life only in the commendatory sense in which we stress the quality or highlights of an existence, instead of the full dimensions, the breadth, depth, and length, of it. Moreover, he maintained that such spirituality is of value only to those whose inclinations demand the quiet pleasures of understanding at cognitive distance from the fray.

These more limited claims are unobjectionable in substance. We can fault them only for emphasis: his frequent celebration of it makes Santayana appear to stress contemplation to the exclusion, or at least at the expense, of other possible perfections. The engaged life so deeply admired by Dewey, for example, featuring commitment to the transformation of nature and society, received virtually no attention, and certainly no plaudits, from Santayana. This does not mean that, should the question have been raised, he would have denied the legitimacy or relative value of such a life. What disappoints is that in his mind, or at least in his writings, the issue did not much arise. Although his persuasive account of the symbolic nature of cognition saved Santayana from the spectator theory of knowledge, his deepest sympathies always remained with the spectator theory of fulfillment.

Final Assessment

Persons who take a literalistic religious view of reality are not likely to accept much of Santayana's philosophy. But they tend also to reject nearly all thought that is preoccupied with modern concerns: with a search for the foundations of knowledge, the challenge of established values, and the attempt to accommodate the findings of science. Those with a sympathy for religious values but uncommitted to doctrinaire views, on the other hand, may find that their best hope lies with Santayana or a system closely similar to his. For, though he declined to believe that religion and theology give us the literal truth about the world, he nevertheless retained their essential insights as deeply accurate symbolic indications of the human condition.

From the philosophical point of view, it is clear that Santayana's system does not have the profound originality of the thought of such early masters as Plato and Aristotle, on which he so heavily relied. It is a late product in the history of human consciousness, which makes striking and wholesale novelty difficult to achieve, but offers in its place the possibility of a vision that is rich, balanced, and mature. This is exactly what we find in Santayana. His system, at its best, represents as high a level of thought as we have attained in the twentieth century. It is sensitive to the full range of human experience and responsive to the most stringent demands of consistency, comprehensiveness, and good sense. In spite of current neglect, it will stand as a major achievement of thought, one of the great philosophical systems and, in private reflection, a permanently attractive home for many minds.

Notes and References

Chapter One

1. George Santayana, *Scepticism and Animal Faith* (New York: Dover, 1955), ix. *SAF* hereafter.
2. Ibid., 7.
3. Ibid., vi–vii.
4. Ibid., viii.
5. George Santayana, *Realms of Being* (New York: Scribner's, 1972), 282. *Realms* hereafter.
6. Ibid., 21.
7. Ibid., 48.
8. Ibid., 829.
9. See Douglas M. MacDonald, "Santayana's Undivided Soul," *The Southern Journal of Philosophy* 10 (Summer 1972): 237–252.
10. See Justus Buchler, "One Santayana or Two?" in *Animal Faith and Spiritual Life: Previously Unpublished and Uncollected Writings of George Santayana with Critical Essays on His Thought,* edited by John Lachs (New York: Appleton-Century-Crofts, 1967), 66–72.
11. Printed in G. E. Moore, *Philosophical Studies* (London: Harcourt Brace, 1922), 1–30.
12. *Realms,* 845–853.
13. Daniel Cory, *Santayana: The Later Years* (New York: Braziller, 1963), 74–76.

Chapter Two

1. Santayana's discussion of scepticism occupies the first ten chapters of *Scepticism and Animal Faith.* Chapter 11, entitled, "The Watershed of Criticism," constitutes the transition to Santayana's own philosophy of animal faith, which is developed in the remaining sixteen chapters.
2. *SAF,* 15.
3. Ibid., 42.
4. Ibid., 97.
5. Ibid., 271.

Chapter Three

1. For a more detailed discussion of these issues, see John Lachs, "Belief, Confidence and Faith," *The Southern Journal of Philosophy* 10 (Summer, 1972): 277–285.

2. *Realms,* 202–03.
3. *SAF,* 266.
4. Ibid., 228.
5. Ibid., 227.
6. *Realms,* 202.
7. *SAF,* 164ff. Also, George Santayana, "Literal and Symbolic Knowledge," in *Obiter Scripta,* edited by Justus Buchler and Benjamin Schwartz (New York: Scribner's, 1936), pp. 108–150.
8. *Realms,* 233.
9. *SAF,* 138.
10. Ibid., vi.
11. Ibid., 305.

Chapter Four

1. *SAF,* 275.
2. Ibid., vi.
3. Ibid., 121.
4. Ibid., 71.
5. For a wonderfully clear discussion of these and related concepts, see *SAF,* pp. 270–71.
6. *Realms,* 293–94.
7. Ibid., 286.
8. John Lachs, "Matter and Substance in the Philosophy of Santayana," *The Modern Schoolman* 44 (1966): 1–12.
9. *SAF,* 271.
10. *Realms,* 827.
11. These chapters are now available in print in John and Shirley Lachs, eds., *Physical Order and Moral Liberty* (Nashville: Vanderbilt University Press, 1969), 139–159.
12. *Realms,* 572.
13. *SAF,* 172–79.

Chapter Five

1. For an explanation of these, see John Lachs, "Two Concepts of God," *The Harvard Theological Review,* 59 (1966), 227–240.
2. George Santayana, "The Philosophy of Mr. Bertrand Russell," *Winds of Doctrine* (New York: Scribner's, 1926), 138–154.
3. George Santayana, *The Life of Reason: Or, The Phases of Human Progress* (New York: Scribner's, 1953), 7.
4. George Santayana, "Normal Madness" in *Dialogues in Limbo* (New York: Scribner's, 1926), 36–57, contains a wonderful discussion of the insanity of conscious human life.

Chapter Six

1. Bertrand Russell, *Portraits from Memory, and Other Essays* (New York: Simon & Schuster, 1956), p.97.
2. George Santayana, *Platonism and the Spiritual Life* (London: Scribner's, 1927), 30.
3. See the chapters entitled "Distraction" and "Liberation," in *Realms,* 673–767.
4. See George Santayana, "Ultimate Religion," in *Obiter Scripta,* edited by Justus Buchler and Benjamin Schwartz (New York: Scribner's, 1936), 280–297.
5. *Platonism,* 83.
6. *Realms,* 845.

Chapter Seven

1. George Santayana, "A General Confession," *The Philosophy of George Santayana,* edited by P. A. Schilpp (Evanston and Chicago: Northwestern University Press, 1940), 17.

Selected Bibliography

PRIMARY SOURCES

1. Collected Editions

The Works of George Santayana. Triton Edition. New York. Charles Scribner's
Sons. 1936–1940. 15 volumes. An incomplete, limited edition of 940
copies signed by the author.

The Works of George Santayana. Herman Saatkamp, Jr., General Editor. Cambridge, Mass., MIT Press. 1986–. This is the definitive, critical edition
of essentially all of Santayana's finished literary output. Twenty volumes
are planned.

2. Relevant Philosophical Works

*Animal Faith and Spiritual Life; Previously Unpublished and Uncollected Writings
by George Santayana with Critical Essays on His Thought.* Edited by John
Lachs. New York: Appleton-Century-Crofts, 1967.

"Apologia Pro Mente Sua," *The Philosophy of George Santayana. The Library of
Living Philosophers,* II. Edited by Paul Arthur Schilpp. Evanston and Chicago: Northwestern University Press, 1940, 495–606.

Character and Opinion in the United States. New York: Charles Scribner's Sons,
1921.

Dialogues in Limbo. New York: Charles Scribner's Sons, 1926.

"The Efficacy of Thought," *Journal of Philosophy, Psychology, and Scientific Methods,* 3 (1906): 410–412.

"A General Confession," *The Philosophy of George Santayana. The Library of
Living Philosophers,* II. Edited by Paul Arthur Schilpp. Evanston and Chicago: Northwestern University Press, 1940, 1–30.

The Idea of Christ in the Gospels or God in Man. New York: Charles Scribner's
Sons, 1946.

The Idler and His Works and Other Essays. New York: George Braziller, 1957.

The Life of Reason; Or, The Phases of Human Progress. I. *Introduction and Reason
in Common Sense.* New York: Charles Scribner's Sons, 1905.

The Life of Reason; Or, The Phases of Human Progress. II. *Reason in Society.* New
York: Charles Scribner's Sons, 1905.

The Life of Reason; Or, The Phases of Human Progress. III. *Reason in Religion.*
New York: Charles Scribner's Sons, 1905.

The Life of Reason; Or, The Phases of Human Progress. IV. *Reason in Art.* New
York: Charles Scribner's Sons, 1905.

The Life of Reason; Or, The Phases of Human Progress. V. *Reason in Science.* New York: Charles Scribner's Sons, 1906.

"Living Without Thinking," *Forum,* 68 (1922):731–35.

Lotze's System of Philosophy. Edited by Paul G. Kuntz. Bloomington: Indiana University Press, 1971.

Obiter Scripta. New York: Charles Scribner's Sons, 1936.

Physical Order and Moral Liberty. Edited by John Lachs and Shirley Lachs. Nashville, Tenn.: Vanderbilt University Press, 1969.

Platonism and the Spiritual Life. New York: Charles Scribner's Sons, 1927.

Soliloquies in England and Later Soliloquies. New York: Charles Scribner's Sons, 1922.

The Realm of Essence; Book First of Realms of Being. New York: Charles Scribner's Sons, 1927

The Realm of Matter; Book Second of Realms of Being. New York: Charles Scribner's Sons, 1930.

The Realm of Spirit; Book Fourth of Realms of Being. New York: Charles Scribner's Sons, 1940.

The Realm of Truth; Book Third of Realms of Being. New York: Charles Scribner's Sons, 1938.

Scepticism and Animal Faith. New York: Dover Publications, 1955.

Three Philosophical Poets. Garden City: Doubleday and Co., 1953.

Winds of Doctrine. New York: Charles Scribner's Sons, 1926.

3. Autobiography

Persons and Places. New York: Scribner's, 1944. First volume of Santayana's autobiography.

The Middle Span. New York: Scribner's, 1945. Second volume of the autobiography.

My Host the World. New York: Scribner's, 1953. Concluding book of Santayana's account of his own life.

Persons and Places. Edited by William G. Holzberger and Herman J. Saatkamp, Jr., with an introduction by Richard C. Lyon. Cambridge, Mass.: The MIT Press, 1986.

Critical edition, in one volume, of the autobiography. This is the first volume of *The Works of George Santayana.*

SECONDARY SOURCES

1. Biography

There are to be two biographies of Santayana. The first, by John McCormick, appeared in 1987. The second, by Richard C. Lyon, who knew Santayana, is scheduled for completion at a later date.

Cory, Daniel, *Santayana: The Later Years.* New York: George Braziller, 1963.
McCormick, John. *George Santayana.* New York: Knopf, 1987.

2. Bibliography
Saatkamp, Herman J., Jr., and John Jones. *George Santayana: A Bibliographical Checklist, 1880–1980.* Bowling Green, Ohio: Philosophy Documentation Center, 1982.
    Immensely useful, exhaustive listing.

3. Critical Studies
It is surprising that, although Santayana is a major American philosopher, there are relatively few books devoted to the study of his thought. This bibliography lists the most significant among these.

Ames, Van Meter. *Proust and Santayana: The Aesthetic Way of Life.* Chicago: Willett, Clark, 1937.
    A fruitful comparison.
Arnett, Willard E. *George Santayana.* New York: Washington Square Press, 1968.
    Good general introduction.
———. *Santayana and the Sense of Beauty.* Bloomington: Indiana University Press, 1955.
    Strong stress on the aesthetic in Santayana.
Ashmore, Jerome. *Santayana, Art and Aesthetics.* Cleveland: Press of Western Reserve University, 1966.
    Art as the key to Santayana's work.
Butler, Richard, O. P. *The Life and the World of George Santayana.* Chicago: Regnery, 1960.
    A picture of Santayana taken from a great distance.
———. *The Mind of Santayana.* Chicago. Regnery, 1955.
    Account by someone not basically in sympathy with Santayana's thought.
Duron, Jacques. *La Pensée de George Santayana: Santayana en Amerique.* Paris: Nizet, 1949.
    Major French work.
Howgate, George W. *George Santayana.* Philadelphia: University of Pennsylvania Press, 1938.
    Consideration of his life and thought.
Kirkwood, Mossie May. *Santayana: Saint of the Imagination.* Toronto: University of Toronto Press, 1961.
    Admiring look at Santayana's achievement.
Lamont, Corliss, ed. *Dialogue on George Santayana.* New York: Horizon Press, 1959.
    Varying perceptions of Santayana's positions.

Lind, Bruno. *Vagabond Scholar: A Venture into the Privacy of George Santayana.* New York: Bridgehead, 1962.
> Personal attempt to penetrate to the heart of Santayana's view of the world.

Munitz, Milton Karl. *The Moral Philosophy of Santayana.* New York: Columbia University Press, 1939.
> The moral vision as central to Santayana.

Munson, Thomas N., S.J. *The Essential Wisdom of George Santayana.* New York: Columbia University Press, 1962.
> General appreciation and criticism.

Reck, Andrew J., and John Lachs, eds. *Special Issue on Santayana. The Southern Journal of Philosophy* 10 (Summer, 1972).
> Contains a hitherto unpublished short essay by Santayana and seventeen papers by various hands on aspects of his philosophy.

Schilpp, Paul Arthur, ed. *The Philosophy of George Santayana.* Evanston and Chicago: Northwestern University Press, 1940.
> Essays by eighteen commentators with a response by Santayana.

Singer, Beth J., *The Rational Society: A Critical Study of Santayana's Social Thought.* Cleveland: Press of Case Western University, 1970.
> Well-crafted account of Santayana's view of politics and social life.

Singer, Irving. *Santayana's Aesthetics: A Critical Introduction.* Cambridge: Harvard University Press, 1957.
> A sensitive introductory work.

Sprigge, Timothy L. S. *Santayana: An Examination of His Philosophy.* London and Boston: Routledge & Kegan Paul, 1974.
> Major study of Santayana's philosophical thought.

Stallknecht, Newton Phelps. *George Santayana.* Minneapolis: University of Minnesota Press, 1971.
> A short appreciation.

Recent work on Santayana is covered in *Overheard in Seville,* the bulletin of the Santayana Society. It is edited by Angus Kerr-Lawson, Department of Pure Mathematics, University of Waterloo, Ontario, Canada N2L 3T2, and Herman J. Saatkamp, Jr., Department of Philosophy, Texas A&M University, College Station, Texas 77843.

Index

111, 113, 114, 115, 116, 117, 137,
138, 144, 146
Ipse, 36

James, William, 5, 10, 130
Jesus Christ, 119–20
Journal of Philosophy, The, 6
Judeo-Christian God, 119

Kant, Immanuel, 21, 23, 30, 46, 95
Knowledge, 17, 18, 22, 27, 29, 30,
35, 37, 38, 39, 42, 43, 44, 54–55,
56, 57, 58–59, 64, 70, 72–73, 74,
75, 76, 77, 78, 79, 84, 88, 89, 100,
117, 118, 119, 122, 123, 127, 140,
147

Language, 9, 72, 111, 127, 128
Lewis, C. I., 6
Life, 112–13
Life of Reason, The, 12, 16, 24, 89,
93, 95–103, 111–12, 132
Life of Reason, The, (Santayana), 6, 19,
22, 61, 101, 124, 131
Literalists, 122, 147
Literary Psychology, 58, 92
Locke, John, 81
Logical Empiricism, 136
Loman, Willie (Arthur Miller), 21
Lotze, Herman, 5
Lowell, Robert, 4
Lucifer, 97
Lucretius, 16, 64, 67, 118, 129

Materialism, 3, 13, 22, 47–48, 52, 53,
61, 65, 73, 74, 89, 112, 123, 142
Matter, 7, 9, 13, 14, 15, 20, 30, 41,
61–85, 90, 92, 94, 116, 119–21,
126, 135, 138, 139, 140, 143, 144
Medieval Philosophy, 48
Memory, 58
Metaphysics, 13, 14, 15, 21, 44, 46,
88, 118, 121, 135
Mill, John Stuart, 101
Mind, 2, 12, 13, 14, 15, 18, 22, 25,
30, 40, 41, 43, 46, 47, 49, 50, 51,
53, 56, 57, 60, 65, 72, 75, 76, 77,
78, 79, 81, 83, 86, 100, 108, 112,

117, 118, 119, 120, 122, 135, 141,
143–45
Mind-Body Problem, 39, 52, 55, 86–
93, 108, 143–45
Modern Philosophy, 142, 147
Modes, 48
Moore, G. E., 22, 64, 94, 125
Moral Life, 7, 11, 13, 95, 102, 107,
116, 118, 123
Morality, 10–11, 12, 40, 60, 63, 68,
86, 89, 91, 93, 94–103, 104–6,
107, 109, 119, 120, 123, 129, 130,
132, 145–47
Moral Relativism, 11, 12, 16, 22, 104–
6, 131, 145–46

Natural Body, 13
Natural Kinds, 10, 70
Naturalism, 6, 19, 30, 42, 53, 64,
114, 118, 120, 121, 128, 129, 135
Nature, 7, 12, 13, 14, 22
New Testament, 119
Nicene Creed, 25, 120–21
Nicomachean Ethics (Aristotle), 13
Nietzsche, Friedrich, 71
Nirvana, 111

Object of Intent, 84
Object of Intuition, 84, 85
Occam's Razor, 136, 137
Old Testament, 119
On The Soul (Aristotle), 21
Ontological, 9, 12, 20, 21, 22, 52, 55,
57, 61–85, 94, 98, 119, 120, 124,
125, 133, 135, 136, 138–39, 143,
144

Parallel Development, 144
Parmenides, 24
Parmenides (Plato), 10
Perception, 31–34, 46, 75, 83–85
Perry, R. B., 6
Pessimism, 3, 15, 17, 74, 104
Phenomenology (Hegel), 19
Philosophy, 1, 7–9, 11, 14, 15, 26, 29,
30, 31, 37, 39, 41, 42, 44, 47, 53,
59–60, 84, 85, 88, 89, 95, 102,
106, 114, 118, 121, 123, 124–47